THE MEDIA AND THE CONGRESS

CONTENTS

FOREWORD By Jonathan Moore   ix

1   **The Fourth Branch, Then and Now**
      A Paper by Douglass Cater   1
          Congressional Status Quo
          The Media's Effect
          The Fundamental Dilemma

2   **The Media and the Open Congress**
      A Paper by Norman J. Ornstein   7
          The Closed Congress
          New Members, New Rules
          The Changing Media
          The Open Congress
          Consequences
          Conclusion

3   **Congress's Complaints**
      A Roundtable   21
          Superficiality and Negativity
          A Responsibility Beyond Reporting
          The Press As Bulletin Board
          The Legacy of Closed Doors
          Conflict Over Substance

Congressional Culpability
Blaming Congress's Problems On the Press
Intended Chaos
What Falls On the Cutting-Room Floor
Congress Versus the White House
Log-Rolling and Arm-Twisting
Keeping Score on Congress

4 The Media's Complaints
A Roundtable   39
Television's Special Impact
The Showhorse Dilemma
The Shrinkage of Washington on Television
The Big Rock-Candy Mountain
News With an Impact on Readers
Making Information More Accessible
An Individual Response
The Demise of Clearcut Issues
Different Media, Different Missions
The Press's Responsibility
It Ought to Be Difficult
A Problem of Democracy
Television the Opinion-Maker
Three Audiences
The Problem of Many Voices

5 The Ingredients of Congressional News
A Case Discussion   61
Introductory Note
Star-Studded Hearings
Parochial Stories That Become National
Using Television to Get Print Coverage
When to Avoid Publicity
Reporting Campaign Contributions
Conflict As News
Frank Church and the Soviet Brigade
Handling Leaks
Four Economic Stories
Media Resources

CONTENTS

6 Covering Tax Legislation
A Case Discussion — **79**
  Introductory Note
  Change in Climate
  The Honeymoon Problem
  Was Wall Street Surprised?
  Riverboat Gamble
  Uninterested Audiences
  Role-Playing
  Different Standards for Television
  A Radical Change
  Following the Leader
  Safe-Harbor Leasing
  Winning by Losing
  Too Much at Once
  Using the Press to Lobby
  Unfinished Business

7 News Judgment and Congress
A Speech by Senator Bob Dole — **101**
  The Majority Difference
  The Access Dilemma
  Prime-Time Amendments
  Untold Stories: Social Security and the Deficit
  The Camera's Impact
  Questions

8 Findings and Recommendations
A Summation — **109**
  Media Findings and Recommendations
  Prime-Time Congressional Debates
  The Economics of Network Television
  Printing Roll-Call Votes
  Cross-Media Criticism
  Congress Findings and Recommendations
  Opening Congress Up
  Bringing Television Producers to Congress
  Educating Home-State Reporters
  Much Ado About Nothing

Media and Congress as Co-Conspirators
Expertise By Subscription
Objective, Not Adversarial

APPENDIX
Major Issues in Congress— Media Relations   125
A Topical Outline by Stephen Bates

FOREWORD

by Jonathan Moore
Director, Institute of Politics
John F. Kennedy School of Government,
Harvard University

The Institute of Politics has two purposes in publishing this book.

First, we want to identify and examine the special character and challenge of coverage of the Congress by the news media as distinct from the press-politics relationship in other domains, such as political campaigns or the executive branch. The interests and constraints which Congress and congressmen together with media organizations and journalists must confront in doing their respective jobs in perpetual interaction deserve more serious consideration than they usually get.

Second, we hope to provide material useful in teaching journalism and government students at the college and graduate levels. Too frequently, at least where Congress is concerned, the study of governmental institutions and of journalism both fail to analyze the dynamic relationship between the two and the impact in both directions.

Four years after the discussions which constitute this book took place, the House and Senate and the networks and newspapers are struggling with the same issues, processes, and constraints in trying to practice and report on politics, respectively. Tax legislation, deficit-fighting, aid to insurgents, war powers, and lobbying excesses reappear in the news. Legislators are still complaining about superficial and sensational coverage; and, reporters are still exasperated about labyrinthine processes and closed-door decision-making. Both remain locked in the same dependency and competition, organizational and political constriction, and commitments to constituents and consumers.

Joel Havemann, a reporter for *The Los Angeles Times* writing in October, 1983, about the conference which produced this book, quoted Democratic Congressman Tom Downey of New York: "The reporters run the spectrum from the very competent, the ones who can cut through the polemics and baloney, to those who only understand polemics and baloney." And Havemann himself observed that the reporters who cover Congress (a) generally believe, given the constraints under which they operate, they "do a fair job of informing the public," and (b) leave the public "with an inadequate understanding of the complexities and nuances of congressional activity." Nothing here has changed.

Yet Norman Ornstein, who is a contributor in this book, recently pointed out why the subject-matter addressed in the following pages has become of greater relevance because of change. In the second Reagan term, tax and budget policies are being resolved by congressional leadership rather than set by presidential initiative, requiring an alert and sophisticated press to interpret the consequences of that change. While the new C-SPAN channel moves to cover the Senate as well as the House, network television has opted out of the process. And individual members of Congress and lobbyists alike are using their own advanced media techniques, experts, and strategies to influence voters in reelection campaigns and votes in legislative battles.

In this book, the discussions among congressional principals, staff and lobbyists, print and television reporters, and political scholars treat symbiotic versus adversarial phenomena, institutional versus individual behavior, integration versus fragmentation pressures, Washington policymaking versus state and district politicking. The commentators in this volume are interested in the inherent difficulties in media coverage of Congress, the designs and impacts each side has on the other, the complexity in organization and process, and the problems of access and production. Does television require special standards of evaluation to match its special constraints on coverage? Are reporters who cover congressional campaigns back home knowledgeable enough about what happens on Capitol Hill? How does the public posturing of members obscure the real action beneath the surface? How does the media agenda affect legislative behavior? All these questions will remain vivid and vital for a long time to come.

The Institute of Politics and *The Los Angeles Times* co-sponsored the conference on *The Media and the Congress* from October 28 through 30, 1983, at the John F. Kennedy School of Government, Harvard University. Without the conference, there wouldn't be a book, and without *The Los Angeles Times*, there wouldn't have been a conference. Seventy-four congressional actors, journalists, academics and staff gathered for seven sessions over three days to explore the inherent difficulties in covering such a decentralized institution as the Congress, to discuss how journalists and congressional actors affect each other's performance, and to consider what the goals of congressional coverage might be and how these goals might be better advanced by those involved. The *Times* and the Institute also co-sponsored a February 1980 conference on "Nominating a President: The Process and the Press." Both contributed to the development of Harvard's new Joan Shorenstein Barone Center on the Press, Politics and Public Policy.

We have Tom Johnson, William F. Thomas, Dennis A. Britton, John Foley, Nancy Tew, William Schneider, and Bart Everett from *The Los Angeles Times* to thank for their manifold contributions to this book. From the Institute of Politics, we are grateful to Charles Trueheart, Betsy Pleasants Whitehead, Carolyn Fontaine, Betsy Northrup, Sarah Farnsworth, Diane Pliner, and Mary McTigue for their fine help.

J. M.
June, 1986

THE FOURTH BRANCH, THEN AND NOW

A Paper by Douglass Cater

A quarter-century ago I was a backseat driver in the Washington press corps as a correspondent for a fortnightly periodical, *The Reporter*. Before most of us had heard of Marshall McLuhan, I watched the press watching government and wrote *The Fourth Branch of Government*. A great many of my journalistic colleagues took umbrage at my calling them the fourth branch. They felt it somehow sullied the vestal virgin image of the press that they chose to claim. I thought I honored the press by calling it a fourth branch—not derived from the other three branches—with rules and organizing principles all its own.

In my book I described the uniquely powerful role performed by the press in the American system of government when compared to Britain's or the Soviet Union's. I concluded that this power derived not as editorial arbiter but, more fundamentally, as gatekeeper of the flow of information within and beyond the Washington community. Washington officialdom—from the president to the lowliest congressman—had adapted to the organizing principles and news definitions of the media. I quoted Walter Lippmann's classic, *Public Opinion*: "Nothing affects more the balance of power between Congress and the President than whether the one or the other is the principal source of news and explanation and opinion."

CONGRESSIONAL STATUS QUO

That was in 1958. Twenty-five years later, we should reexamine these propositions as they pertain to the media and Congress. Let us begin with certain basic assumptions about the governance of Congress which would prevail whether or not the press existed:

- To speak of *the* Congress is to misspeak. Ever since Woodrow Wilson we have known that Congress was a disintegrate institution. When we have talked about periods of congressional ascendancy, we have talked about periods in which particular internal arrangements of power in Congress have made it possible for Congress to challenge the executive power. By no means has Congress been an integrated, purposeful institution in wielding power.
- During periods in history when Congress was judged to hold ascendancy over the president, it was the hierarchs, the tyrannical Speaker, the unfettered committee chairmen, the arbitrary committee fiefdoms that constituted the effective use of congressional power, not the coherent and concerted will of the body as a whole.
- The schizophrenia of the congressman as statesman versus servant of his constituents is no more resolvable today than it ever was.
- The separated powers of Congress give special incentive to the congressional entrepreneur to find reward, spiritual or venal, by working in the interstices of the policy process.
- Neither the president nor the Congress has been a respecter of strict definitions of role. Each continually asserts claims over the territory previously assumed to lie within the other's domain. The Supreme Court has shied away from enforcing its definition of roles except on rare occasions—e.g., Truman's seizure of the steel mills or, more recently, Congress's exercise of the legislative veto—when it has read the Constitution to the other two branches.

All the above assumptions, I say, would likely be valid even if elected representatives in Washington communicated to the people by smoke signals rather than through the sometimes-smoky translations of the media. What, then, is significant about the media in their relation to Congress?

THE MEDIA'S EFFECT

A quarter century ago, my concern was that in the coming communication age the habits of the media were exacerbating the disintegrate nature of Congress, exaggerating the role of representatives who seek to exploit image over substance, and creating a distorted and ofttimes false picture of the reality of the struggle between the president and Congress. In brief, my contention was that the press was compounding inherent difficulties of Congress in sticking to its role as the principal repository of legislative power within the American constitutional system.

It should be remembered that I wrote during the dark shadows of the McCarthy era. To quote myself at the time: "McCarthy represented something quite new in the history of the American demagogue. The traditional demagogue could be measured by how skillfully he sized up and played on fears and prejudices existing within a region or a social group. McCarthy's skill, on the other hand, lay primarily in his capacity to stage a single issue so as to dominate the channels of communication and to distract a national audience. He was never terribly good before a large crowd. But he knew how to rule the headlines."

Beyond the cynical manipulations of McCarthy, I was disturbed by the shift of the workload of Congress, which was motivated, I suspected, by the power of publicity in the new age of communication. Nowhere in the Constitution is there any mention of legislative oversight as a function assigned to Congress. Yet there was exponential growth of time and attention devoted by committees and subcommittees to reviewing executive decisions, usually without any intent other than to make headlines, not laws.

This could be justified as performing an essential service for the people's right to know. Yet during both the Truman and Eisenhower eras, of which I wrote, it served to distract the people as well as their elected leaders from more paramount problems of governing the nation. A graduate student at the Kennedy School might one day catalogue the amount of space and time the media devoted to the staged congressional hearings of trivial importance. Yet the hearings, however trivial, contributed to the public's impression that Congress, not the president, was in Lippmann's phrase "the principal source of news and explanation and opinion."

Has anything changed since 1958? On the positive side, the crude demagoguery of the McCarthy variety has not flourished in an age of expanding communications. But I am still troubled by the temptations—on Capitol Hill and in the White House—to employ subtler forms of demagoguery when debating the hyperbolic issues of strategic armament or, for that matter, the state of the economy. I still wonder whether the media, in their partiality toward those who leak rather than those who proclaim, may be stimulating this demagogy.

We face inherent difficulties of press coverage of Congress. These mostly relate to the question of whether reporting all of its parts can ever approximate the reporting of Congress holistically. Like the blind men and the elephant, there is a fundamental dilemma of which piece of the anatomy to grasp. Publicity, the reverse side of the coin called news, has been known to re-create congressmen, for better or worse, even as Hollywood re-creates the star to fit an image.

How does the reporter make known all the complexities to his reader as he tries to relate the story of Congress? In 1923, Walter Lippmann described the reporter's impossible function as being that of "the umpire in the unscored baseball game." Have we made any advances in trying to keep score? Better newspapers now devote much more space to investigative journalism and in-depth analysis. Television brings the live congressman into the living room. But the congressional baseball game continues to be waged much as Lippmann described it.

In the age of the computer there have been remarkably few advances in digesting the vital information about Congress. There is nothing in political coverage comparable to network television's marvelous use of technology and data retrieval to provide coverage of major sporting events.

THE FUNDAMENTAL DILEMMA

The fundamental dilemma is that the good congressman's job is to participate in the building of a consensus that leads to serious legislative purpose. The good reporter's job is to tell the story before the consensus has been reached and to inform as many people as he can, even if it prevents consensus-building. I don't know that there can be any reconciliation of that difference in role.

Lippmann, while still a comparative newcomer to journalism, reached a pessimistic conclusion about the limits of the news process. "If we assume that news and truth are two words for the same thing, we shall, I believe arrive nowhere," he wrote. The function of news, by his definition, is "to signalize an event," whereas the function of truth is "to bring to light the hidden facts, to set them into relation with each other, and to create a picture of reality on which men can act." Lippmann ridiculed the notion that the press, "by acting upon everyone for a few minutes each twenty-four hours can create a mystical force called Public Opinion that will take up the slack in public institutions." His final book attempted to define a public philosophy adequate to the governance of a free society while recognizing the severe limits of informed public opinion.

Nearly two centuries ago, during the growing pains of our republic, John Adams despaired over whether the art of governance had advanced even one iota since the time of Darius. The cause for despair continues now that the task of governing seems more formidable than ever. Some congressmen may avoid despair by confining their picture of reality to the short-term needs of their constituents or the narrow domain of their committees. Some reporters, clinging to the vestal virgin stereotype of journalism, may find satisfaction in simply "telling it like it is." The rest of us, I strongly suggest, must continue to seek ways of discovering and communicating a picture of reality on which men and women can act.

THE MEDIA AND THE OPEN CONGRESS
A Paper by Norman J. Ornstein

One purpose of this conference is to explore the interrelationships between Congress and the mass media—what each side wants from the other, and how these competing and/or symbiotic desires affect, among other things, both Congress's public policy and the public's perceptions of Congress.

The subject is not an easy one to address. There is not *a* Congress: There is a House and a Senate, each very different in its internal structure and its media coverage. There are, besides these two institutions, 540 individual members with their own career demands and media needs and relationships. Obviously, too, there is not *a* mass medium. There are a variety of electronic media, from television networks to local television stations to radio outlets. On the print side, there are national outlets, including the wire services and a handful of national newspapers and newsmagazines, and there are local newspapers and some local news bureaus. In addition, there are the important but invariably neglected specialized media, including trade papers, newsletters, and magazines like *Congressional Quarterly* and *National Journal*.

To avoid writing a hundred-page monograph, I have chosen to bring these elements together in some rough fashion by focusing on change. Congress and its media coverage have both changed dramatically over the past fifteen years. I'll explore how and why they have changed, and in the process shed light on their interrelationships. Readers, especially those who've been around the

Capitol longer than I, will note that there is some necessary oversimplification and hyperbole in the descriptions. I apologize in advance.

THE CLOSED CONGRESS

Through much of the postwar period, at least up to the mid-1960s, Congress, especially the House of Representatives, was a closed system. Its significant operations—votes, mark-ups, and strategy sessions—were in large part conducted behind closed doors. The policy agenda was predominantly in the hands of the chairmen of the standing committees, who had the power to dominate their bodies: controlling the subcommittees, through their jurisdiction over membership and chairmanships; hiring and firing the staff; deciding when and on what subjects the committees would meet. Their selection was automatic, and they were virtually immune from removal or retribution. Party leaders also had considerable authority. They acted as brokers between committee chairmen, and between the barons and the rest of the chamber; they managed and orchestrated the floor agenda; they held a great deal of sway over rank-and-file members through control and selective use of perks and punishments. Rank-and-file members went along to get along, because virtually all the incentives for those concerned about their congressional careers existed *inside* the chamber. An overseas junket, a luscious committee or task-force post, an additional staffer, a slot on a conference committee, a role as a floor manager of a bill, a water project for one's district, a bill considered in committee—the routes to a successful congressional career were internal ones, controlled by the leaders.

The mass media tended to reinforce this system. Through the 1940's and 1950's, coverage given to Congress was limited. This was especially true for television, of course: In the era preceding the thirty-minute nightly news, there was little time and scarce resources to devote to Congress. There was little incentive, too. Right up to 1970, with rare exceptions, virtually all the House proceedings were closed to television cameras. The Senate did permit selective broadcasts of committee hearings, and at times encouraged the live broadcast of committee investigations: Estes Kefauver [D-Tennessee] and organized crime in 1951, Joseph McCarthy [R-Wisconsin] and communism in 1954, John McClellan [D-Arkansas] and labor fraud in 1957, and J. William Fulbright [D-Arkansas] and Vietnam in 1966. But floor proceedings, mark-ups, and most key committee deliberations were off-limits for television.

Print media gave more coverage to Congress, but it was selective and limited. The national print media had full-time congressional reporters, but they understood and lived by the congressional system as well as by the conventions of journalism. Congress was largely portrayed in terms of the committee barons and party leaders, often based on the information they provided (frequently off-the-record). Junior members were by and large neglected, except to supply gossip about behind-the-scenes horsetrading and wheeling and dealing. Congressional scandal, with occasional exceptions like Adam Clayton Powell [former member of Congress, D-New York] was downplayed, while drunkenness, sexual byplay, or other malfeasance was ignored. True, much of the muckraking coverage of Congress as an institution was negative: criticism for scuttling civil rights bills, for blocking presidential initiatives, for perpetuating an outmoded seniority system. But this was neither pervasive nor relentless, and it presented little threat to the system as a whole.

Local media coverage of Congress was limited, to say the least. With the exception of major metropolitan dailies, few local newspapers, radio stations, or television stations maintained a significant Washington presence. Except for the wire services' coverage, there was little news about individual members in their own districts. Lawmakers could shape local coverage with press releases, media events, and so forth, but not many members of Congress had full-time press secretaries to do so. Also lacking were such electronic devices as beepers and videotape to provide an instantaneous liaison with home electronic media.

What did this media coverage mean? Congress, because its key internal deliberations were ignored and because outlets for coverage of rank-and-file legislators were minimal, saw its stable, predictable, contained, and closed system preserved, even reinforced. As long as the key decisions were made behind the scenes, and not open to public scrutiny through media attention, those members who had a near monopoly of resources and an edge in the rules enhanced their power. Many individual lawmakers, who got little individual media attention back home and lacked the resources to create or to command more, often found themselves in precarious electoral positions—positions that could best be improved by getting the perks available to those who followed the congressional barons.

NEW MEMBERS, NEW RULES

By the mid-1960s, Congress was beginning to change, first in its membership, due in part to political trends triggered by the 1964 election and in part to a natural generational shift emerging through retirements. Through the 1970s, Congress became both younger and more junior.

The membership changes strained the closed congressional system in three ways. The growing juniority directly threatened a system dominated by seniority, with its highly hierarchical and top-heavy power structure. Secondly, the change in membership affected the ruling Democratic Party. There had been a longstanding delicate and even balance between the southern and northern wings of the party, in overall numbers and in power positions. As the South became more party-competitive and as Democrats improved their electoral position in other regions, the balance in numbers shifted, but the seniority system held the power relationship stable. In other words, northern Democrats gained in numbers but lost in relative power—a clear formula for disaffection and agitation. Finally, the late 1960's and early 1970's saw a different kind of legislator elected. Many had no prior elective or political experience; even more had little or no party background. Political training came as often as not from the anti-Vietnam war movement. Large classes of aggressive, assertive, and anti-establishment newcomers were not going to be easily assimilated into a system designed to keep newcomers quiet for extended periods of time.

With membership change came rules change, especially in the House. Congress decentralized and democratized, taking power from committee chairmen and spreading it among subcommittee chairmen and rank-and-file members. Committee chairmen were subjected to individual secret ballot votes every Congress, and their powers were decimated. Subcommittees expanded in number and became virtually independent, while subcommittee memberships and chairmanships spread out, removed from the aegis of the full committee chairmen. The subcommittee reforms relied, ironically, on seniority to reduce the powers of the full panel chairmen.

At the same time, committee and office staffs expanded and spread. As part of the subcommittee alterations, professional staffs were allocated to subcommittee chairmen and ranking members, but not in a redistributive fashion; they were simply added to existing personnel. As a result, the number of committee staff employees in the House nearly quadrupled from 1965 to 1980.

In the Senate, where comparable change occurred without explicit structural reform, committee staffs increased by 240 percent in the same period.

Staffs expanded for a multitude of reasons other than the desire to alter internal power arrangements. Not least among them was a growing hostility toward the White House, especially while it was occupied by Richard Nixon. Congress felt that Nixon was leading a concerted assault on the most cherished congressional prerogatives; to respond; the members needed more armaments. Thus, personal staffs and related resources also expanded in this era. In the mid-sixties, each House member was entitled to a dozen staff people, with a salary budget of between $100,000 and $125,000. By 1980, the staff salary allotment was over $300,000 with 22 employee slots. Just as significantly, the amounts allocated for other office resources—including telecommunications, computers, and modern office equipment—also expanded sharply. Consequently, members of Congress were able to handle easily, with more staff and more efficient hardware, greater constituency demands; they could even invent sophisticated and creative ways to expand constituent contact. But each member also had resources left over to add legislative assistants and to create or expand press liaisons. In 1963, the *Congressional Staff Directory* listed only 26 of the 435 House members as having press secretaries. By 1980, barely a fifth of the members failed to list a press assistant.

In the early 1970's, both houses of Congress changed their rules to open up deliberations. Through the 1950's and 1960's, 35 to 40 percent of congressional committee meetings had been closed to the public and the press; this included all committee and subcommittee mark-ups, where bills were put together line by line. Reforms opened these sessions up. *Congressional Quarterly*, which had monitored both open and closed meetings since 1953, abandoned the process in 1975 because there were no more closed meetings to count. The House of Representatives went further to combat secrecy by altering floor procedures to allow open roll-call votes on amendments to bills—votes that had previously been closed, nonrecorded tallies—and to make it easier to get a vote taken on a amendment. The reformers' campaign to end secrecy was aided by active and widespread mass media encouragement and coverage.

THE CHANGING MEDIA

While all these changes were transforming Congress, the mass media were also changing. Beyond any doubt the most significant change was the television networks' move to a thirty-minute nightly newscast in 1963. The half-hour news program confirmed television's growing importance as a major source of information. It also meant a doubling of the news hole to be filled every evening.

In the Senate, as I noted, committee investigations from time to time had titillated television. Senate rules also permitted television access to committee hearings, and the Senate had become more interesting to television after John Kennedy proved it a potential breeding ground for presidents. So Senate television coverage began to increase in the mid-sixties.

In the 1970's, television coverage of the House rose sharply. When the House amended its rules in 1970 to allow television cameras in open committee hearings, coverage of the House increased slightly. For other reasons, television attention to Congress jumped markedly during the ensuing decade. One reason was conflict—a staple in the definition of news. Our political system is based on perpetual conflict, but with an aggressive Richard Nixon facing off against a hostile Democratic Congress, conflict took on new dimensions. There were vetoes, often accompanied by presidential televised addresses or statements and followed by congressional responses. There were military actions in Vietnam, followed by impassioned denunciations from liberal congressional critics and by mass public demonstrations and moratoria that centered on the White House and often led to Capitol Hill. There were frequent occasions of crackling tension—good news and good television.

Good television became great television with Watergate. The Ervin Committee hearings in the Senate [Sam Ervin, former senator, D-North Carolina; chairman, Select Committee on Campaign Activities] were followed by the Judiciary Committee impeachment proceedings. To permit cameras into the Rodino panel [Peter Rodino, member of Congress, D-New Jersey; chairman, Judiciary Committee], the House amended its rules in 1974 to permit television coverage of committee meetings. The story was the impeachment of a president, but it translated into a televised drama surrounding a few dozen obscure members of the House—who turned out to be surprisingly interesting.

Watergate and impeachment brought an unprecedented degree of media attention to Washington, and much of it remained after Nixon's departure. Journalists and editors who had not focused much on Washington discovered Congress to be newsworthy and action-packed—all the more so because of its changes. More, and more aggressive, subcommittees meant sexy, tension-filled hearings. The internal power struggle meant conflict. Congress's resulting openness meant more news access and outlets. And the boom in investigative journalism spurred by Watergate found its biggest potential outlet in and around Congress. Reporters were spurred by the congressional scandals—Wilbur Mills [former member of Congress, D-Arkansas] and Tongsum Park, for example—that followed closely on the heels of Watergate. Scandal and sloth, as well as policy, were meat for coverage on Capitol Hill. The result? Doubling in the number of radio and television correspondents in the congressional press gallery from 1967 to 1981. For print, the growth in numbers was not so dramatic, but it was marked nonetheless—especially because the number of newspapers was shrinking. Pooled news services, like States and Medill, also provided tailored coverage of Congress to newspapers that had never before had it.

Much of the expansion of coverage was local in orientation and relatively resource-poor. This coverage tended to downplay or ignore scandal, eschew expensive investigative journalism, and focus on the activities and reactions of the local congressional delegation. Representatives with press aides, electronic beeper capability, and the use of a low-cost, full-service television-radio recording studio could supply all the reactions local media wanted, at no cost to the media. Local television and radio stations and newspapers got more prestigious Washington reporting; and, in the process, representatives got more media attention back home that they in large part controlled, helping to solidify their electoral bases.

More media attention on Congress meant more opportunity than ever before for individual members to get national publicity. In high-circulation magazines like *People* and *Glamour*, the possibility existed to get a lavish pictorial, just as would a president or movie star. Television shows like *Today, Good Morning, America, Nightline*, and *60 Minutes* expanded their coverage of Washington legislative policy-makers. Opportunities as never before existed for any member, down to the most junior, to get national attention.

It came with scandal: Wilbur Mills, Bob Bauman [former member of Congress, R-Maryland], Charles Diggs [former member of Congress, D-Michigan], Gerry Studds [member of Congress, D-Massachusetts], Michael Myers [former member of Congress, D-Pennsylvania], Dan Crane [member of Congress, R-Illinois], et al.

National prominence also came to members who defied conventional wisdom and conduct. Some denounced party leaders: John Le Boutillier [former member of Congress, R-New York] and Jim Bates [member of Congress, D-California]. Others denounced Congress and their colleagues: Bruce Caputo [former member of Congress, R-New York] and Shirley Chisholm [member of Congress, D-New York]. Yet others slammed Washington: Ed Zorinsky [member of Congress, D-Nebraska] and Paula Hawkins [member of Congress, R-Florida]. Some challenged their own presidents: Dennis DeConcini [member of Congress, D-Arizona] and Newt Gingrich [member of Congress, R-Georgia]. One slept in his office: Jim Jeffords [member of Congress, R-Virginia]. One tried to solve the hostage problem in Iran: George Hansen [member of Congress, R-Idaho]. Another tried to solve our difficulty in El Salvador: Clarence Long [member of Congress, D-Maryland].

Yet other lawmakers got national attention by publicizing issues. Tax cuts: Jack Kemp [member of Congress, R-New York]. Government waste: William Proxmire [senator, D-Wisconsin]. Human rights: Tom Harkin [member of Congress, D-Iowa]. Pentagon waste: Les Aspin [member of Congress, D-Wisconsin]. Abortion: Henry Hyde [member of Congress, R-Illinois]. Nuclear freeze: Ed Markey [member of Congress, D-Massachusetts]. Teenage chastity: Jeremiah Denton [senator, R-Alabama].

Note that Caputo, Le Boutillier, Bates, Denton, Zorinsky, Hyde, Hawkins, and De Concini got themselves in the media spotlight in their freshman terms. Each exhibited the sort of maverick behavior that would not have been tolerated in the closed Congress of yore.

THE OPEN CONGRESS

More media attention combined with new and different members and reforms brought us, then, a different Congress—the open Congress. With meetings, hearings, mark-ups, and votes open to public and press scrutiny, behind-the-scenes wheeling and dealing was curtailed. With resources and staff expanded to every rank-and-file member, with perks like subcommittee assignments coming automatically, and with power dispersed within the committees, formal leaders and chairmen lost their system of sanctions and incentives. No more was it "to get along, go along"; instead, everyone got along.

The open Congress consisted of well-staffed, aggressive members, all participating actively in the process, following every subject area, primed to offer amendments on all bills. Under these circumstances, few bills emerged unscathed. The handiwork of subcommittees and committees was regularly overturned or rendered unrecognizable.

Fewer incentives, then, remained for members to follow the traditional career patterns: wait your turn, work within the process, develop an area of expertise, become a legislative craftsman, aspire to be a chairman or ranking member. New career incentives emerged instead. As I put it elsewhere: "As media coverage expanded, the number of members of Congress who were brought to public attention mushroomed, and more and more of the publicized members came from the rank and file. . . . This trend toward personal publicity provided, in contrast to the Rayburn era, a range of tangible and possible outside incentives. No longer did a member have to play by inside rules to receive inside rewards or avoid inside setbacks. One could 'go public' and be rewarded by national attention: national attention in turn could provide ego gratification, social success in Washington, the opportunity to run for higher office, or, by highlighting an issue, policy success." The nature of the open Congress was expressed well by Senator John Danforth [R-Missouri] in a recent sermon: "For politicians, the key to success is to be in the news."

In the 1980's, however, Congress has shown some signs of closure, or at least of slowing the rate of increased openness. Staff and resource growth have declined, as have the number of roll-call votes and subcommittee hearings. Leadership clout and assertiveness have increased somewhat, as has the willingness of lawmakers to work out deals behind the scenes. The Senate has shown more of these signs than the House, perhaps because it has always received more media attention and thus has felt the costs of openness more acutely. The Senate, too, has continued to resist television coverage of its floor proceedings [until June 2, 1986].

But some things haven't changed, including the scope and intensity of media coverage of Congress. As a result, junior members continue to speak out, and individualistic, media-oriented legislative behavior is still more the norm than the exception.

CONSEQUENCES

This system and the interactions between media and Congress have widespread consequences. For individual members, the consequences have been manifold. Expanded local media coverage, enhanced by the media-related resources available to each congressional office, has considerably improved both the electoral advantage of incumbents and the favorable image of individual legislators. Left largely in the hands of the individual lawmakers, the favorable local coverage has also reduced members' reliance on their party for electoral assistance.

Media opportunities have also provided the necessary condition for outside incentives, and thus for the open Congress. For many individual members, this means more career outlets and openings. But for others, who aspire to careers as insider, legislative craftsmen, the media coverage and the other elements of the open Congress mean heavy costs and disincentives. Why work hard, out of public view, laboriously putting together a piece of legislation if it will be eviscerated on the floor by thoughtless amendments offered by casual colleagues? Why work anonymously at detailed oversight of a complex policy area if your colleagues don't appreciate your efforts, or even ridicule you for them?

For Congress as an institution, the open system has meant more fluidity, less predictability, more motion and less movement. Congress has greater difficulty passing bills, and fewer are passed now than previously. Those that do pass are longer, much longer, and more complex, laden with amendments and superfluous provisions. As the system closes somewhat, we may see somewhat more predictability in scheduling and in voting, fewer floor amendments, more focused laws. But as long as elements of the open system remain, including the media coverage, the change in the institution will not be dramatic.

Public perceptions of Congress are substantially influenced by media coverage. The positive local coverage of congressmen is balanced by largely negative coverage of Congress as an institution. It is a truism nowadays that we love our congressmen and hate Congress; media coverage is one substantial reason.

The nature of national coverage also shapes broader public notions of Congress, frequently reinforcing misconceptions. Readers and viewers of national media may easily be left with the following impressions: Congress is perpetually racked by conflict and ideological combat. Congress is a lazy institution filled with lazy members who take extended vacations called recesses. Congress holds hearings, briefly debates issues on the floor, and does little if anything else. Congress is ridden with scandal, including bribery, drunkenness, sexual misconduct, and plain selfish venality. And it's all much worse than in the past, and getting worse yet.

All of these themes are overstated or just plain wrong. They exist for several reasons. One reason is access. Hearings are open to television, and now, so is the House floor. There are numerous stories in newspapers and on television about junkets and PAC contributions because the records are now compiled and open to the public, and journalists have become practiced at using the files in the office of the Clerk of the House and the Federal Election Commission.

There is also the innate cynicism of journalism. Skepticism about congressional motives—expense accounts, congressional pay increases, reasons for passing or blocking legislation—is natural and in many instances well-founded. But stories about junkets, waste, lecture honoraria, and expenses often dominate congressional coverage.

Another reason is the definition of news. News is conflict and, more and more, news is scandal. Conflict has always been newsworthy, and the more open Congress is filled with palpable conflicts to be covered. Scandal too has long been newsworthy, but it has become much more so in recent times. The definition of news has changed; Michael Robinson documents well the much greater coverage given to recent scandals than to past ones. More coverage is not the only aspect—scandal also gets better placement and more emphasis. What was inside is now front page; below the fold, now above it; twenty minutes into the newscast, now leading it.

Finally, there are journalistic norms. These too have changed. A couple of decades ago, a story of scandal would not have been reported until an indictment was handed down; behind the scenes drinking or carousing was ignored. Today, it is not uncommon to have rumors and vague allegations top front pages or lead newscasts. The best example was the alleged congressional-page sex and drug ring on Capitol Hill. Allegedly involved lawmakers were described on two network newscasts during the preliminary stage of an FBI inquiry. Similarly, preliminary Justice Department probes of cocaine use led to several news stories on Congressmen Barry Goldwater, Jr. [R-California], Ron Dellums [D-California], and Charles Wilson [D-Texas]; none has been charged or indicted.

In an open Congress, media coverage of this sort leads to certain kinds of behavior by individual members. If you denounce colleagues involved in an alleged scandal and criticize the institutional response to the charges, you are virtually certain to get extensive media attention; witness Bruce Caputo on Koreagate and Newt Gingrich on the page incidents of Messrs. Studds and Crane. If you use your subcommittee to hold a hearing that will involve fireworks with an administration official (Toby Moffett [member of Congress, D-Delaware] and Anne Gorsuch [administrator, Environmental Protection Agency]) a corporate executive ("Scoop" Jackson [former senator, D-Washington] and Exxon President Clifford Garvin), an interest group official (Jeremiah Denton and Planned Parenthood representatives), or one of your colleagues (Orrin Hatch [senator, R-Utah] and Ted Kennedy [senator, D-Massachusetts]), you are likely to get media coverage and in the process make a point, spotlight your name and presence, or highlight an issue. If you spend your time marking up a tax bill, you get neither attention nor credit.

Congress has certainly provided opportunities and access to media, especially national media, to get these stories and to get them out. Yet the open Congress, reflecting perhaps the continuing ambivalence of a formal leadership that cut its political teeth in the old closed system, does not welcome the mass media with entirely open arms. Perks for reporters, from well-located parking to office space to preferred seating in Capitol restaurants, are balanced by restrictions, often nonsensical ones on camera access, even for still cameras, and stand-up locations. The Speaker will not allow cameras on the House floor at any time, even when the Chamber is not in session, and the fixed cameras covering the House floor are controlled by the House itself. The Senate has been even more restrictive, and in the process it has precluded much sensitive and knowledgeable journalistic treatment of its action and role. Locations for television stand-ups are limited to a handful which restrict the subject and thrust of the lead-in used by television reporters.

Moreover, congressional leaders, in spite of the fact that they and the Congress would doubtless benefit from more media attention to the ins and outs of the legislative process, have done little to encourage journalistic access to or understanding of the limits and possibilities of Congress. Howard Baker [senator, R-Tennessee] is an exception here: He realizes that television coverage of the Senate floor would mean more than 30-second sound bites on the evening news (though these 30-second segments are not necessarily all bad). Shows like the *MacNeil-Lehrer NewsHour, the Lawmakers, Nightline,* and *Sunday Morning* would be tempted to show longer excerpts from floor debate, much more than they have of the House. And there would probably be some gavel-to-gavel coverage from time to time of critical debate on an arms control treaty or a budget, which would show well-prepared legislators engaging in serious discussion of an important topic—better prepared and more thoughtful, of course, because of television coverage.

Other leaders, however, are shying away from media because of its effects on the open Congress. They have put mark-up sessions and conference committees in broom closets, discouraging television coverage. They have failed to brief reporters on upcoming events of legislative, as opposed to publicity-related, significance. They have failed to find ways to translate internal elements or genuine policy debates into news stories. Leaders have not tried to help journalists find good stories about legislative craftsmen, or to create the conditions where such people and their issues can get more and better coverage.

CONCLUSION

What should be done? Let me briefly suggest a few things. First, I would like to see journalists covering Congress rethink their definition of news. The real work of Congress, the key actors involved, and the complex and delicate interplay in the process can be conveyed, and conveyed in an entertaining fashion that hits home with readers and viewers. Repeated stories about junkets, recesses, and pay raises need not be so frequent or prominent. Our ridiculous preoccupation with scandal or bare hints of it can be downplayed.

I would like to see members of Congress think about ways to change the internal incentives, adding to those of the workhorses and reducing those of the showhorses. We will not soon, if ever, return to the closed system of yore, but there are probably ways to strike a better balance. More leadership control over floor proceedings, a higher threshold to obtain roll-call votes on amendments, modest additional committee control over subcommittee activity, and fewer committee and subcommittee assignments would be steps in the right direction.

3

CONGRESS'S COMPLAINTS
A Roundtable

PARTICIPANTS

Stephen H. Hess (moderator), senior fellow, Brookings Institution; author, *The Washington Reporters*
Richard E. Cohen, congressional reporter, *National Journal*
Barber E. Conable, Jr., member of Congress, R-New York
Richard F. Fenno, Jr., Kenan Professor of Political Science, University of Rochester; author, *Home Style: House Members in Their Districts*
Charles D. Ferris, attorney, Mintz, Levin, Cohn, Ferris, Glovsky and Popeo; former general counsel, Senate Democratic Policy Committee; former chairman, Federal Communications Commission
Bill Frenzel, member of Congress, R-Minnesota
James P. Gannon, editor, *Des Moines Register*
Paul Houston, congressional correspondent, *Los Angeles Times*
Gary Hymel, executive vice-president, Gray & Co.; former press secretary to Speaker of the House Thomas P. (Tip) O'Neill (D-Massachusetts)
Arthur Maass, professor of government, Harvard University
James McCartney, national correspondent, Knight-Ridder Newspapers
Charles McDowell, Washington columnist, *Richmond Times-Dispatch*
Joan McKinney, Washington correspondent, *Baton Rouge Morning Advocate and State Times*
John K. Meagher, vice-president for government relations, LTV

Corporation; former staff minority counsel for the House Committee on Ways and Means
Roger Mudd, Washington correspondent, NBC News
David R. Obey, member of Congress, D-Wisconsin
James B. Pearson, former senator, R-Kansas
Carole Simpson, Washington correspondent, ABC News

STEPHEN H. HESS: If you've been unfairly attacked by the liberal/conservative news media, if your words have been taken out of context, if your privacy has been violated, if the correction never caught up with the story, this is your opportunity.

The way I will proceed is to try to get our problems or complaints on the table by asking people from the Congress side what disturbs them the most. Then we will broaden it with fuller explanations of the complaints. We will then open it to the press, but I don't think they will get quite equal time; their panel is next. And then we'll turn to Dick Fenno and Arthur Maass for what scholars are paid to do, bringing out the meaning and the patterns.

Okay, Dave Obey: What is it that you hate the most about the way the press covers Congress?

SUPERFICIALITY AND NEGATIVITY

DAVID R. OBEY: In terms of the way much of the press, especially the networks, cover the Congress, the number-one problem is superficiality. They emphasize the conflict rather than the true mood of the House on many issues. Often, especially on institutional as opposed to issue-oriented questions, coverage is almost purposefully negative and pejorative—for example, CBS's *60 Minutes* piece on the Congress, done by Harry Reasoner [aired October 16, 1983].

On the issue-oriented level, an example is the way all three networks covered the Lebanese vote [on September 29, 1983]. In spite of the fact that the institutional question at hand was whether Congress would be locked in, in terms of future options in Lebanon, the networks played it in terms of whether there should be an immediate pull-out or an eighteen-month commitment. They played the extremes and ignored most of the debate because the main issue at hand was not that visually exciting or that emotional.

MR. HESS: Simplistic, conflict, negative, play extremes. Bill Frenzel, could you add to that list?

BILL FRENZEL: My problem is that the news that I read and watch—and I don't watch very much—seems manufactured. Instead of reporting news, the press is inventing news, and trying to make it exciting, trying to sell an extra ad or grab a headline.

Also, the press—which has only discovered the Congress in the last decade—uses the Congress as an attempt to embarrass the president. I am never consulted on my views, nor are my colleagues. I'm always expected to say something nasty about the president. I am badgered; words are put in my mouth. The president happens to be of my party. I'm sure David had the same thing when President Carter was in office.

Another problem that bothers me is that the press thinks it can only report events. Congress is not an event, it is a process. Either the press doesn't understand that, or it assumes the public doesn't understand it.

I have a little problem with what I call the cheap-shot syndrome as well. I have a splendid daily in my district. I have been on its front page three times—once for growing a mustache, once for shaving off a mustache, and once for reporting my taxes late. I suspect that I have done something more significant in thirteen years, and that they are probably aware of it.

Just one other example. I would say that William Proxmire [senator, D-Wisconsin] has probably done some wonderful things in his time in Congress, but the Flying Fickle Finger of Fate Award [Golden Fleece of the Month Award] was not one of them. And yet that's one of the few things that I can remember the press covering in his long career in Congress.

MR. HESS: Barber Conable, have you any complaints?

A RESPONSIBILITY BEYOND REPORTING

BARBER CONABLE: My complaints are fairly general and, I'm afraid, they are almost inherent in the way a free press operates.

In that respect I find the man-bites-dog syndrome is a real affliction. What makes news is the exception and not the rule. And, clearly, what also makes news is what feeds public suspicions and the basic negativity about representative government. Thus, if ten congressmen are misbehaving, the public thinks the condition is epidemic and forgets that there are 425 others who are living with their wives, keeping their hands out of the cookie jar, and probably doing a good job of trying to represent their constituencies.

The problem is that the press is an essential ingredient in the dialogue of representation. It means that we are almost instinctively on the defensive about our function and our institution, through the mass communication that's necessary if people are to have any understanding of what's going on in Washington.

The press does have to take some responsibility for accurately describing institutions and not just feeding people's doubts about them. As long as representative government is going to be based primarily on a dialogue between the members and their constituents, and as long as the press is going to be an inherent part of that process, they have to have a responsibility beyond reporting the news.

MR. HESS: Gary, in all of those years of watching it from the Speaker's office, how did it look to you?

GARY HYMEL: Of course, the Speaker has no problem with access to the press. He has a press conference every day.

I would say, though, that at least three-quarters of the members of the House never talk to a national press person. They don't trust national reporters. They run every two years and a misquote or a misstep can be fatal to them, so they duck the national press.

The other point I want to make is that staff people's complaint generally is that reporters are lazy. They won't come into a committee, talk to the staff director, get background on a bill, and try to understand the issue. They are looking for the sensational quote or the piece of film that creates sensation. Or they just come up to a staff director and ask about the good witnesses or the good confrontations. And they base their research, not on trying to understand the problem and trying to explain it to somebody, but on getting the quick quote and the chance to satisfy the editor.

MR. HESS: John, from the point of view of the staff of a major committee of the House, what did the coverage look like to you? What is your complaint, if any?

JOHN K. MEAGHER: I don't know that I have as much a complaint as an observation.

It seems to me we have gone through a history of closed sessions and then open sessions, and now we are going back to closed sessions. It's difficult to get things done in a committee like Ways and Means when you have a lot of people who get up in front of the press and make a lot of speeches. In reaction to that, Congress has gone back to writing the bills behind closed doors.

That's a question that everybody has to think about—why it has happened and whether it's a good result. From the inside it's nice to be able to write those laws without sitting out in the open, because you just don't have the same kind of pressure. On the other side, it seems to me as a lobbyist now that the process has become terribly closed, but maybe that's just my perspective.

MR. HESS: Charlie Ferris, from the Senate leadership side, how did it look to you?

THE PRESS AS BULLETIN BOARD

CHARLES D. FERRIS: Senators generally have far less problem with access to the national press, and they feel more comfortable dealing with it. The senators like to think that they deal with the cosmic and that the parochial is left to the House. Therefore they feel more confortable talking about national issues.

From the leadership standpoint one element of the daily press—the *Washington Post, New York Times,* and *Los Angeles Times,* which are read on Capitol Hill—was a very useful forum to communicate among the leadership of the Senate. The leadership used to communicate a great deal through the press. What spin the story had was very important in setting the environment for the next day's action.

The press is certainly no different from every other institution. They are very human, they have prejudices, they have viewpoints, and their choices of adjectives convey those viewpoints. But that's part of the dynamic. To some degree one attempts to influence the vocabulary that certain writers use when they write their stories.

MR. HESS: Jim Pearson, be our clean-up hitter.

JAMES B. PEARSON: We were admonished to stay away from the question of competency, but I want to return to it, though not so much in measures of intelligence or appetite for work.

In 1975 in the Senate we went through five or six acrimonious weeks debating decontrol of natural gas. It later passed a compromise in 1978. Right after that debate the Columbia School of Journalism had an article in its publication [*Columbia Journalism Review*], which I understand is widely accepted. It said that in this debate, there were probably no more than about ten or twelve senators who really understood the dynamics of the natural gas industry. But they were more concerned by the fact that there probably weren't more than half a dozen or a dozen people in the press gallery who understood enough to report it properly.

At a time when you are going into questions of energy, of weapons systems, of economics and budgets, somehow or other the Senate and the press are going to have to return to a more specialized age. It's all very well for the guy sitting up there from the *Oil and Gas Journal* to understand what it's all about and to report back to the pros. But this was an issue that needed great public education, and it just wasn't there.

MR. HESS: Members of the media, you have been called simplistic and negative. You deal in manufactured news and only in events. You've been known to take cheap shots and feed the doubts of the people. You have been called lazy and your competency has been called into question.

Roger Mudd, have they left anything out?

THE LEGACY OF CLOSED DOORS

ROGER MUDD: Most of us at the table grew up covering Congress and learning to stand outside closed doors, knowing we weren't really wanted inside and suspecting the worst. We knew that there were such things as unrecorded votes because congressmen didn't want their names listed. We knew that congressmen changed positions and then issued press releases to cover up.

And so I think the negativism is as much a fault of Congress as it is of the press. Because there was so little air circulating, particularly in the House, we were left to try to reconstruct events as they happened on the floor, particularly for television. That's an imperfect way to report. And when Mr. Frenzel says that we discovered the Congress only ten years ago, it was only about ten years ago that the Congress really wanted to be covered in any intensive way.

Finally, I would ask who is responsible for the Fickle Finger of Fate Award. Is it the media, or is it Senator Proxmire himself? It's not our award, it's his.

MR. HESS: You've been called simplistic. Charlie McDowell, you put out a program called *The Lawmakers*. A lot of people think it's a pretty fine program. What has happened when you've tried to go beyond simplicity?

CHARLES McDOWELL: That kind of puts me on the side of the people speaking for Congress, and that makes me terribly nervous.

The Lawmakers is an effort on national public television to cover the process—not to be trivial or confrontational, but to really cover how it works. America's great industries have not rushed forth to support mild, thoughtful coverage of Congress that tries to meet these charges. There has been no voluntary support from great educational institutions. Every time you get to an intellectual city you find the program is played, not at 8:30 at night when it's sent out, but after midnight. It's very frustrating to try to cover the process with these obstacles.

A consultant talking to us about the program said that the confrontational aspects of Congress must be emphasized if we want support and viewership. So maybe we can blame the public and go home.

MR. HESS: Jim Gannon, when I went around the country to check with some editors on their Washington coverage, I found few who were happy with reporters. They seemed to think reporters had gone native or were unguided missiles. Do you want to fire the shot back into Washington, or accept the blame right where you are in Des Moines?

CONFLICT OVER SUBSTANCE

JAMES P. GANNON: I'm tempted just to plead guilty to all charges and throw myself on the mercy of the court, but I want to respond to a couple of things. I'm uncomfortable, too, because I've got to agree with many of the comments that have been made by the people connected with Congress.

Gary hit on something very important when he talked about the essential laziness of the press. The press in general does a marvelous job on the conflict and the confrontation—and it's overdone—but we do a terribly poor job on the substance of the legislation or the issue. That is our greatest failing. I don't think you can blame it on the public by saying that they won't read it. If you do it well, they will read or watch what's going to happen to them as a result of a tax bill or natural gas deregulation. But I don't think we do that very well.

Now that I'm in an editor's position and see what comes from Washington, particularly from the wire services, I don't think we do a good job in that regard. When I want a good story that explains a bill—such as the unisex insurance bill which is currently before the Congress, where all we have heard is the women's groups making one charge and then the insurance industry making another charge—I have to ask my Washington bureau to look into it and explain it to me. Then I can get a good story.

MR. HESS: Jim McCartney, are you going to plead no-contest too?

CONGRESSIONAL CULPABILITY

JAMES McCARTNEY: No, I plead guilty across the board. There's no charge that's been made here with which I do not agree and about which I am not appalled.

When I was working for a college newspaper some years ago, I could never find out the substance of legislation; it was always presented as a horse race in the reporting out of Washington.

That's still true. In handling a bill, the press will give it a label, usually a cliche, and that label is used forever after by the headline writers and reporters. And nobody ever finds out what's in the bill. The question is, what do you do about it? I think that's what we ought to be focusing on.

From the reporter's point of view, Congress does one lousy job in making it possible to find out anything in an intelligible way. If you ever go to a meeting of the Senate Foreign Relations Committee, you get a bunch of speeches by politicians trying to get into the paper in the most hopelessly childish way, and very little discussion of the substance of the legislation or the problem.

You have to turn this thing around, those of you on the congressional side. There is incompetence, no question about it—though if I were speaking on the congressional side it's an issue I wouldn't raise. But we are not idiots. We are able to digest a fantastic amount of information if it's presented in an intelligible form.

MR. HESS: Joan McKinney, you're one of a great number of regional correspondents and you're telling people in Baton Rouge about their delegation. Are you folks so good at covering it that no one is mad at you?

JOAN McKINNEY: I think regional reporters may be the worst at covering the institution as an institution. Covering the process probably is not the kind of assignment we get from home.

I want to talk about two things that Gary and Charlie raised that cause many regional reporters to feel vulnerable.

You said that the majority of the House never talks to the national press. The people most of the House are ducking the national press for, are their home-town reporters. But sometimes there's an assumption that they can present their story to the home-town reporter in their way, their words, and that is how it's going to get in the paper. If you are a lazy and incompetent reporter, it may get through in that form, but that attitude is somewhat simplistic.

You also talked about the leadership seeking out the national press. They do that. The only people who really need me are those people in my congressional delegation, and so I sometimes have a problem of access to other members. They do not need me.

MR. HESS: Paul, what does it look like from covering the state with the largest congressional delegation?

PAUL HOUSTON: I'm going to be self-serving and defensive, and plead not guilty to most of these charges, at least for the people I run around with—the *New York Times, Washington Post, Boston Globe, Baltimore Sun, Chicago Tribune.*

The kind of reporting I read and I am involved with is a hell of a lot more sophisticated. I think we do deal institutionally without taking cheap shots at perks. Sure, we cover sex scandals and drugs when they come up, because over the last ten years we have gotten ethics committees for the first time in the history of Congress. But that makes up maybe one percent of the news.

And as for the charge we are not issue-oriented, I would call your attention to the natural gas coverage in the *Wall Street Journal, New York Times, Washington Post.* I found that to be well informed, and I know the reporters covering it were pretty darn sophisticated on the subject.

BLAMING CONGRESS'S PROBLEMS ON THE PRESS

RICHARD E. COHEN: I want to question the basic premise which comes from several of the members here and also pervades the academic literature: that the problems with Congress seem to be caused by the press. I'd suggest that at least some of the problems with Congress are caused by Congress.

Let's take two recent issues in which a case can be made that Congress has not held itself out in great glory: budget and tax issues. I think most members of Congress, including the Ways and Means Committee member sitting at this table [Barber Conable], agree that Congress needs to do something about raising taxes and cutting spending, but their committees have not produced such legislation. The press hasn't done all that well in reporting those issues, but I don't think it's the fault of the press that the legislation has not been forthcoming. It's been suggested that a certain spinelessness within Congress has produced that lack of action. That's Congress's problem, not the press's problem.

Yes, a lot of criticism of the press that has been voiced at this table and in the literature generally is valid. But so what? Is that really what's wrong with Congress? And is the press coverage of Congress the reason for the public's rather low view of Congress?

MR. HESS: I hate to be the one with the most mundane thoughts on this panel, but twenty-odd years ago I was on Tom Kuchel's [former senator, R-California] staff. We answered a lot of mail, we took care of a lot of constituents' problems, and we thought we were making a special contribution in helping the people of California through the maze of the bureaucracy. I can't recall anybody writing much about that. Is that so uninteresting a topic?

MS. McKINNEY: It's not uninteresting, and in fact it often makes a good human-interest story. What you're talking about is constituent service that to us sometimes seems politically self-serving.

MR. FRENZEL: Speaking from the congressional viewpoint, we don't need news coverage about that. That isn't news; that's our job. We have plenty of weaponry of our own in that regard—and it's abused and overused, as everybody here knows. But I think that is not a fair indictment of the press.

MR. McDOWELL: If you wish to see the Congress become defensive and uncooperative, talk to a congressional office about its letter-writing operations and constituent service. They are embarrassed to death by the fact that they give ninety percent of their time to that mail, and the more mail they answer the more mail they get and the more staff they hire.

MR. OBEY: Charlie, I've received over 40,000 letters on just one issue this year. I got almost 160,000 letters and postcards from my district, mostly garbage generated by Washington lobby operations, but nonetheless creating a political necessity to respond. How would you suggest we go about that?

MR. McDOWELL: I'm suggesting that you encourage us to write about it and try to discuss this new relationship of the Congressman as ombudsman to the constituent.

MR. OBEY: Let me tell you why we don't want television to do that—most of my comments have been related to television. Because if you try to give institutional and political-science answers to questions, such as Tom Downey [member of Congress, D-New York] tried to do with *60 Minutes*, you get a *National Enquirer* framework. You take a bath if you try to deal with it, frankly.

MR. McDOWELL: I have no answer to that.

MR. HESS: Carole, speak up for television.

CAROLE SIMPSON: I'm going to try.

One of my biggest complaints covering the Hill was not being able to get stories on the air. I don't decide what story is going to be on the network news, and I don't decide how much time I can devote to that story. That is up to the producers. And reporters are fighting that battle with producers all the time. For example, I was covering the Civil Rights Commission and the attempt by the Senate to reach a compromise on the president's appointees. I absolutely could not get that on the air. Of course, Grenada and Lebanon came along. There's great competition for news time. Without the commercials, there's twenty-two minutes to devote to everything that has happened in the world.

MR. HESS: We have mostly House members here, and yet no one has complained that all you reporters are over in the Senate.

MR. OBEY: I'd rather keep them in the Senate.

MS. SIMPSON: I think there is a sense, at least at the network level, that the Senate is the more important body and the breeding ground for presidential candidates.

MR. MUDD: Absolutely. The media regards most senators as potential presidents and gravitates toward them. And most of them are.

INTENDED CHAOS

MR. FERRIS: I always felt Congress was working best when it was in apparent chaos. That atmosphere usually means that everyone is actually focusing on an issue that reflects basic values. I don't believe in the notion that ten members of the House should decide for the other 425. That's how it used to work in the 1950s, when Sam Rayburn [former Speaker of the House, D-Texas] took care of the House while Lyndon Johnson took care of the Senate. Congress worked very efficiently. Two men took care of 535 very diverse viewpoints. I don't think that's how it's supposed to work. When there's really fighting and chaos—the press can contribute to that and they should—I think it works well. That's how it should work.

MR. HESS: I want to ask the people on the House side a question. In a sense all the media people here are from Washington, but that doesn't represent all the media people by any means. Say something about that other part of the media you deal with constantly back in your districts. Have they become a larger force?

MR. CONABLE: I had a problem in my district because I sensed that very few of the reporters thought of me as a human being engaged in a human exercise. They saw me as an assignment. They stuck a mike in my face, asked a question, and left. So I started having an off-the-record press luncheon at the beginning of each year. I invited all the people that covered me back home. I met with them and said, "I'm Barber Conable, here's my job in Congress, here's my perception of what's happening." I tried to have an interpretive discussion with them. And I must say, it has greatly improved my relationship with the press back home. I had to take the initiative on it, because otherwise I would have continued to be nothing but an assignment, very dimly understood. All they knew was that I had a job somewhere off in the distant seat of government.

I do worry about the interpretive role in representative government generally, and who is going to carry that burden. Our perception of ourselves is altogether too much that we are not leaders but representatives. We have a horrid saying: "If you have to explain anything, you're in trouble." Or, "If you find yourself floating in a pool of economic illiteracy, don't try to drink the pool, just swim prettily."

Somebody ought to be trying to put it all together. The interpretive role of the press is largely neglected. They focus on the movement and the controversy and the conflict, which generally is part of the environment but not necessarily part of the substance. If people are going to understand what representative government is all about, then somehow we have to get a partnership here to do more interpretive work. That requires the congressmen to take some initiative.

One other point. I've never done a television interview that lasted less than twenty minutes, and I've never had more than half a sentence used on a television show. It's because they are not looking for an interpretation of the issue. They have a point of view, and they are looking for that half-sentence that will fit in with the viewpoint they want to express.

WHAT FALLS ON THE CUTTING-ROOM FLOOR

MS. SIMPSON: I disagree with that.

MR. CONABLE: What happens to the other nineteen minutes? Maybe it wasn't flashy enough.

MR. MEAGER: They only have twenty-two minutes for the whole program.

MS. SIMPSON: I object to your saying they have a point of view and are looking for the answer that will fit that point of view.

MR. CONABLE: The whole story has to fit together. If I don't say what fits into the story, you can be sure it will wind up on the cutting-room floor.

MS. SIMPSON: Congressman Conable, don't you agree that conflict is news and that process is not necessarily news?

MR. CONABLE: Yes.

MS. SIMPSON: What would you have us do, ignore the conflict?

MR. CONABLE: No, but accept some broader responsibility. Part of your responsibility should be an interpretive role to help people understand more than just the conflict.

MS. SIMPSON: Aren't you encouraged we have things like Cable News Network and *Nightline*?

MR. CONABLE: That's great. I'm astonished at the number of legislative junkies out there watching absolute chaff hour after hour.

MR. FRENZEL: I'm amazed at the number of people who watch that awful stuff, who reporters claim don't have time to understand the issues.

MR. CONABLE: And who are thirsty as the dickens for it.

MR. MUDD: What awful stuff?

MS. SIMPSON: C-SPAN.

MR. FRENZEL: The House of Representatives in action.

MR. HESS: You have said that the Senate gets more attention than the House, though the House members don't seem as troubled by that as some others might be. Does the majority party get more attention than the minority?

MR. CONABLE: Sure, they have more power.

MR. MEAGHER: You have to recognize what Roger does is headline news. You're asking him to interpret stuff when he has twenty-two minutes to cover the world.

In the case of minority-majority, you always get the chairman because he has the power. Beyond that, you get the star. Conable gets on because he's glib. But somebody else doesn't get on because they are not articulate or they don't say something that's cool, though they may be very smart. I think that's the distinguishing characteristic. So I look upon what the networks do as showtime. It is a show they put on every night, and that's fine. The stuff that they do is a totally different kind of journalism, and the standards ought to be different. I think what we have done here today is mix apples and oranges.

CONGRESS VERSUS THE WHITE HOUSE

MR. HESS: Another thing that I haven't heard, and yet outside this room it's talked about often, is that the White House seems to dominate media attention. Is anyone from Congress upset about this?

MR. CONABLE: Clearly that's part of the development of television as a major medium of communication. You can't put 535 members of Congress on every time you put the president on, so the president is going to dominate the airwaves to a very substantial extent. I think you can correlate the growth in the power of the president as an opinion-molding force with the development of television. I'm not sure there's any answer to that. The babble of many voices is always going to be considerably more diffused than somebody who speaks from a bully pulpit.

MR. McCARTNEY: What the White House does, of course, is spoonfeed us. It's very easy. You go over there and you sit and everything's predigested. They have essentially planned a program to get on the evening news. That's all they think about all day; the whole machine is geared to that one objective. They are writing half the script of the evening news before Roger is out of bed.

Now, your problem in Congress is that you haven't any organization at all. It is a babble. I think it's wonderful. But you have to find some better ways to present information to this screwed-up medium that I represent. And you have to make it even simpler for Roger's medium.

MR. McDOWELL: But how is Congress going to respond to the White House, maintain some position against the White House, without a Sam Rayburn or a Lyndon Johnson swaggering?

MR. FERRIS: Congress doesn't have a position until they vote. They are a bottom-line organization. There are 535 opinions; there is no single congressional opinion until they vote.

MR. McDOWELL: And they vote on the agenda that the president sets down. They sit there in their wholesome babble without the chance to help shape the agenda.

MR. CONABLE: They are different functions. What's wrong about the president's having an inherent advantage? After all, a president is bound to be a leader. To a certain extent we are representatives. We are not leaders but people saying, "Hey, wait a minute," or, "I don't know whether my guys will go along with that." That's our role, not the role of grabbing the public eye by providing the initiative.

MR. McDOWELL: So I'm in a weak position as a citizen for wishing that you could present a congressional point of view at a time like this?

MR. FRENZEL: I think you are. That's the point I made at the very beginning. You keep looking for a confrontation between Congress and the president. Occasionally the Congress agrees with the president. It must be a matter of great disappointment to the press, but it happens.

MR. HYMEL: There's one matter no one has mentioned. I don't think the press understands the two-year term. In fact, nobody understands the two-year term except the congressman who has to vote in peril every time. A congressman has to keep his ear to the ground, read editorials, and call back home and ask what they're talking about. And here come reporters from the national press who want to cover the great big issues—there's a constant conflict.

Also, all they ever do in Congress is compromise. The press doesn't understand what a human institution it is, and they hate the word "compromise." Right away they think you're compromising morals and principles. But that's not what congressmen are doing. They are doing the art of the possible, yielding and maybe making deals—"I'll support your amendment if you'll support mine." They don't trust the press to understand that and report it back home.

MR. MUDD: I think that's one thing the press does understand.

MR. HESS: Professor Maass, what's your view?

LOG-ROLLING AND ARM-TWISTING

ARTHUR MAASS: Many reporters begin with the assumption that decision making in the Congress is more decentralized than in fact it is. This enables them to focus on the behavior of individual congressmen and on deals that they make rather than on the outcomes of decisionmaking in committees and on the floor. Furthermore, the reporting itself has a decentralizing effect, as Barber Conable has suggested. Let me, then, offer evidence showing that the decentralization assumption is not necessarily correct.

Take, for example, legislation that authorizes the government to conduct certain programs and projects. Is Congress more concerned with individual projects in members' districts or with national program policies? Some years ago in giving a seminar on Congress at the Kennedy School, I made the statement that in legislation for the development of airports, Congress's principal concern had been with broad standards and criteria for deciding how and where it would be appropriate to spend federal money, rather than with approving individual airports. A student responded that I was wrong, that Congress's principal concern was with individual airport projects in members' districts. "I know," he said, "I am the legislative liaison officer for the Federal Aviation Administration, and much of what I do every day is answer phone calls from congressmen who want to know about projects in their districts." To resolve the issue I suggested that this experienced student read the legislative histories of all of the authorization and the appropriation bills for the airport program for the last ten years. He read thousands of pages of hearings and reports, and he found in them only references to three airports. In other words, I was right. In their role as legislators members were concerned about standards and criteria. What, then, were all of those phone calls? After Congress passed an authorization bill and then appropriated money in lump sum to carry it out, congressmen called to ask if projects in their districts were eligible to receive money. In doing this they were performing constituency service; but this wasn't part of the legislative process at all. Failure to distinguish between the constituency service and legislative activities of Congress is, I believe, a principal source of misunderstanding and misreporting the national legislature.

Another example: The reporting of Congress frequently plays up log-rolling and pork-barreling as principal decision modes of the body. Actually Congress is absolutely terrible at these techniques; they tend to generalize every program so that as many states and districts as possible can participate. And they are especially suspicious that the executive may try to buy support from local and special interests by favoring certain districts and regions over others.

There is also a great deal of misreporting of legislative liaison—that is, efforts by the president to build support for his programs in Congress. There has been much talk in this room, for example, about Reagan's economic victories in 1981, when he persuaded a significant number of Democrats to support him while holding together the Republicans in Congress. The *Washington Post* said that "in a flurry of last-minute arm-twisting President Reagan and his aides cut deals right and left" to win. But their story missed the big point. The firm foundation for the president's victory was not these so-called deals, but the remarkable popularity of the man and his ideas among voters and legislators. Capitol switchboards were jammed with calls supporting the president. The president's principal arguments with members to whom he spoke were that the election had given him a mandate for the general substance of his program, and that he believed there was popular support for it in the members' districts. I do not mean that presidents and cabinet officers never offer appointments or projects to influence Congressmen's votes, but that this is not a primary tool of legislative liaison, and that its use is dramatically overstated by the press.

I asked a knowledgeable faculty friend here at Harvard why so much of the media missed the big story and instead played up wheeling and dealing. His response was, "That's what these reporters were taught when they took college political science in the 1950s." So let me conclude by assuming, on behalf of my professorial colleagues, responsibility for any misperceptions you may have.

MR HESS: Dick Fenno, wind things up.

KEEPING SCORE ON CONGRESS

RICHARD F. FENNO, JR.: When professors don't have knowledge, they make distinctions. Let me make a distinction. I like the notion in Douglass Cater's paper about scorekeeping. The media are the scorekeepers, and they do at least two kinds of scorekeeping. One I call institutional scorekeeping. That's where the press describes and evaluates progress toward some legislative outcome. Here, it seems to me, the power of the press is the power to allocate praise and blame. The other kind of scorekeeping is what I call individual scorekeeping. That's where they describe and evaluate the activities of individual legislators. Here the power of the press is to make judgments as to whether legislators are doing a good job, whether someone is a good House member or a good senator.

The media do a better job at institutional scorekeeping than they do at individual scorekeeping. I spent a year hanging around the Senate Budget Committee, and I became enormously impressed with the job that the regular budget beat people did. I could not have understood what was going on if it had not been for the reporting, slogging through the detail day after day, by Helen Dewar [*Washington Post*], David Espo [*Associated Press*], Marty Tolchin [*New York Times*], Paul Houston, David Rogers [*Boston Globe*], Bob Merry [*Wall Street Journal*]. They reported accurately, they highlighted the essential conflicts and decisions, they charted the progress of the budget.

The media have always done a better job at institutional scorekeeping, and my guess is that their desire to do a better job helped create the open Congress. For example, the media's interpretive work on the seniority rule was highly persuasive to members of Congress in reforming the rule. The press is really the mirror that Congress holds up to itself, and it holds it up every morning.

Why is it that the media are better at institutional scorekeeping than at individual scorekeeping? There are two reasons.

One is that individual scorekeeping is a new part of the job. The open Congress has created the need for it. You've got a lot of highly entrepreneurial, highly individualistic members of Congress, trying to push their own activity through the press. Basically you've got several hundred members singing "Hey, Look Me Over" to the press. That's a new thing and it creates a booming, buzzing confusion. I'm not surprised that the press would have difficulty grappling with this problem, but they have to grapple with it. They have to do individual scorekeepig because that's what the new Congress is about.

The second reason why the media don't do such a good job at individual scorekeeping is because so much of it has to do with what goes on in the home districts. Congressmen's entrepreneurial activity is designed in most cases to appeal back home. The press pays much more attention to what's going on in Washington, and I think that's a misallocation of their resources. Readers have to be given some guidance as to whether their members are doing a good job, and not just from what the legislators tell them. The media, if they are going to cope with the new Congress, have to cope with this question.

It seems to me that the finest hour of the press in covering Congress came during the House Judiciary Committee's impeachment hearings. The media were forced to go back into the home districts to find out what these thirty or so people were like, what was driving them, what was motivating them. In trying to work the Washington-district linkage, they explained to the reader the great diversity of the country, they showed people honestly trying to do what was right, and they showed the procedural constraints under which members of Congress had to work in order to have a genuinely consensus-building institution. They combined institutional scorekeeping and individual scorekeeping.

4

THE MEDIA'S COMPLAINTS
A Roundtable

PARTICIPANTS

Martin A. Linsky (moderator), assistant director, Institute of Politics, Harvard University; editor, *Television and the Presidential Election*
Jacqueline Adams, Capitol Hill correspondent, CBS News
William H. Cable, partner, Williams & Jensen; former deputy assistant to President Carter for congressional liaison
John C. Culver, former senator, D-Iowa
Paul Duke, moderator, *Washington Week in Review*
Alan Ehrenhalt, political editor, *Congressional Quarterly*
Clark Hoyt, managing editor, *Wichita Eagle-Beacon*
Albert Hunt, Washington bureau chief, *Wall Street Journal*
Charles O. Jones, professor of government, University of Virginia: author, *The United States Congress: People, Place, and Policy*
Harry McPherson, partner, Verner, Lipfert, Bernhard & McPherson; former assistant counsel to the Senate Democratic Policy Committee; former special counsel to President Johnson
Norman J. Ornstein, visiting scholar, American Enterprise Institute; editor, *Congress in Change*
Leo Rennert, Washington bureau chief, McClatchy Newspapers of California
David Rogers, Washington reporter, *Boston Globe*
Michael J. Robinson, associate professor of government, Georgetown University; author (with Margaret A. Sheehan), *Over the Wire and On TV: CBS and UPI in Campaign '80*

Peter E. Teeley, press secretary to Vice-President George Bush (on leave); fellow, Institute of Politics, Harvard University

Jonathan Wolman, Washington news editor, Associated Press

MARTIN A. LINSKY: The theme of this discussion is the problems the media have in covering the Congress. We have on this panel a wide range of press perspectives—people who do very different kinds of jobs and who have very different kinds of needs. So let's begin by asking the members of the press to tell what their mission is in covering the Congress—what they see as their job, their prime responsibility, their goal—and then what are the biggest obstacles in achieving it. Then we can move to some of the contributing problems in the Congress.

LEO RENNERT: We have three people in our Washington bureau. Two are assigned full time to cover what we call California-related news. Our papers are the three *Bees* in northern California—Sacramento, Fresno, Modesto. I cover national news, including stories on the Hill.

Getting to the gripe part, I was struck that nobody brought up Vietnam and Watergate in the previous seminar. To me those two things are central to what we are discussing. Twenty-five years ago you may have had a closed Congress, but the press trusted the Congress, individually and collectively, as people who could accomplish something, who knew what they were doing. Because there was a closed Congress, legislators felt that they controlled the press and, therefore, they were comfortable with the press. But now, as a result of Watergate and Vietnam, we have an untrustworthy Congress and, correspondingly, Congress looks upon the press as untrustworthy too. We are at a time now of great basic cynicism and doubt.

In our coverage of the California delegation we look upon the post-Watergate babies as people who have been terribly disappointing, and we have written about that. In many instances people have come in as self-serving careerists under the guise of reform; they are in many respects midgets compared to the people who preceded them. You also have some important and substantive people, and we have not hesitated to point out the positive.

So, I'd like to get away from this open versus closed Congress and the institutional and technical problems. I think we ought to address ourselves more to this question of trust, where we on both sides are still recuperating from Vietnam and Watergate.

TELEVISION'S SPECIAL IMPACT

PAUL DUKE: I think our real mission as reporters, in covering Congress and in covering national politics, is to try to find as much truth as we can and report that to the public. This sounds like one of those grandiose goals, but I feel that it is very basic. Mark Twain once said that Washington is a city that regards truth as a precious commodity and therefore it should be rationed. All of us know a lot of rationing goes on in Washington.

The problem as far as the Hill is concerned—as a reporter who goes back some years and who once worked for a newspaper that really tried to get at the basic truth [*Wall Street Journal*]—is, how do you really discover the truth? How do you cover the Congress? Do you emphasize the grandstanders? Do you report the excitement of the Hill? Or do you try to get below the surface to give meaning to what is really happening there, and dwell on those stories which are really important?

From the television standpoint, we face a lot of problems. One is that a lot of the people who work in television do not understand Capitol Hill. When I was at NBC some years ago, it was not unusual for a producer to dismiss a story idea on the ground that nobody understood it, and it was just another Hill maneuver that people didn't care about. It was hard to sell stories unless they were "exciting"—a fierce clash on the Senate floor or some dramatic film from a Senate hearing, for example. Network reporters still have this complaint.

Another problem is that certain members of Congress are very adept at using the television medium, and you have to guard against people reaping excessive, unwarranted publicity. All too often the real news comes from people who are not particularly adept at using television, who aren't quite as eloquent, who can't make their statements as well as some of the more polished performers.

Trying to get at what's happening on the Hill is difficult, and it's compounded by the fact that there's so much going on at all times. On any given day you might have thirty-five to fifty committee hearings, and one of the difficulties with television is that it can cover maybe two or three of those hearings at best. The cameras go to the ones that are more likely to produce those exciting moments. But in the meantime, frequently, things that affect many people's lives go unreported, or at least not publicized as well as they might be.

Television has come a long way. There are some programs now

that are trying to remedy the deficiencies. The commercial networks are doing a much better job, and I think some of the things we are doing in public television are providing more of a public service. But we still have a way to go.

ALAN EHRENHALT: I don't have some of those day-to-day news problems. I write a weekly column about Congress as an institution. If possible I relate that to things that are going on in the society beyond. Then I edit a book in which we try to evaluate members as legislators.

One problem that I have is sort of a Catch-22 of congressional reporting. If you're there every day seeing people, stories are occurring to you, you're developing the day-to-day relationships, the access is more or less permanent—then you get ten or fifteen inches in the paper the next day or a few seconds on the evening news. You don't have much opportunity to make use of what you find out. Or, if you have a job like mine, where you have time and space, then you lose some of the access and the immediacy that you have working for a daily newspaper. I'm not sure what the solution is. I think you lose a lot either way.

MR. LINSKY: Compounded, if you look at it from the readers' point of view, by the realization that they aren't generally able to get all the perspective and all the immediacy at the same time. They are making choices too.

THE SHOWHORSE DILEMMA

ALBERT HUNT: I did a profile of a "showhorse" five or six years ago. The point of the piece was members who care more about publicity and headlines than process and legislation. I thought it was important to note it was not an attack on one person, but on a type. I mentioned Fred Richmond [member of Congress, D-New York]. He called up quite angry and insisted we have lunch because he wanted to tell me how wrong I was. We had lunch, and he said, "I was on CBS twice last month." I said, "Geez, Congressman, that's the point of my piece." He said, "I put out seventeen press releases, and the *New York Times* has picked up three." I said, "That's what I'm talking about, a showhorse." He said, "Well, look. Let me ask you this. The next time you refer to me, could you refer to me as a semi-showhorse?" That's part of the problem.

The second part of the problem is that we are talking about "the media" here, and that's a misnomer. The problems and criticisms of television and print are quite different. I think that I take a backseat to no one in my admiration for some of the stuff that Roger Mudd did in covering the Congress. But basically the premium in television today is on what has been called "the hyperventilators." It's a lot easier to hyperventilate in front of the White House than it is in front of Congress, and that's why each network has more people covering the White House than the Congress. These quite capable people who do cover the Congress can get on the air only if there's confrontation or scandal.

I think we have to face the fact that television dominates the dialogue in America today. People on my side may not like it, but it happens to be true. If you want a case study, look at what CBS did a year ago on the page sex scandal. It's one of the great case studies of American journalism. I wish we, my side, would spend more time writing about this and about the way television covers institutions like Congress. And I would invite them to do the same about us.

THE SHRINKAGE OF WASHINGTON ON TELEVISION

JACQUELINE ADAMS: I knew I was going to be beaten up. The basic problem is that we are in the midst of a revolution. Certainly at CBS, and I think to some degree at the other networks as well, we are seeing a basic shrinkage of Washington coverage. There are four people covering the White House. There are two people who cover Capitol Hill. The White House isn't getting on the evening news as often, and the Hill gets on even less. From a personal standpoint that bothers me—I'd rather be on the evening news than not—but I can't completely disagree with the judgment call.

MR. LINSKY: Why not?

MS. ADAMS: Instead of covering a hearing in the Russell Building, the show is trying more to get out into America and deal with the people who are affected by the politicians in the Russell Building. We still have to cover the activities on the floor; in many cases we still have to go to the hearings. But the stories on the air are more often done from the field.

Also, you have to sell a story to the editor, and the editor wants action, not process. "Tell me when Congress is going to do something." They are not so much interested in a committee decision; they want final action. And that isn't what Congress is about. Congress is about process. So the two of us on the Hill are constantly beating our heads against a wall, caught in battles both with the sources in Congress and the producers in New York.

MR. LINSKY: So there's a tension between the business of Congress, which may be more process, and the news of Congress, which may be more conflict.

MR. ADAMS: And the business of news. News is just the stuff between the commercials—that's been pointed out to me by my friends in business.

MR. DUKE: Conflict apparently is news, but sometimes resolution of conflict can be more important news. Some years ago at NBC I covered a hearing where George Meany tore into Richard Nixon. It was pretty exciting stuff, as we say in television. On the same day I discovered Wilbur Mills [former member of Congress, D-Arkansas] and Senator [Edward M.] Kennedy [D-Massachusetts] reached a compromise agreement on a national health insurance program. They had been widely apart in their approaches, and it was a very good story. But somebody decided that the film of George Meany was much more exciting. They decided to go with that, and passed up the real news from Capitol Hill that day.

Other reporters from the *New York Times* and the *Washington Post* learned about the Mills-Kennedy compromise the next day. It made headlines all across the country, and then my editors wanted the story. They missed the scoop because they wanted something which really was not news, but which they regarded as good film.

CHARLES O. JONES: Do editors know anything about Congress?

MS. ADAMS: Not particularly, no.

MR. HUNT: That's one area where television and print have a lot in common.

MR. LINSKY: I think it's important to make that point, but let's not take the easy way out by beating up on people who aren't here.

THE BIG ROCK-CANDY MOUNTAIN

DAVID ROGERS: I don't have a lot of problems with Congress. For me Congress is the big rock-candy mountain—all these people who will talk to you, who will explain things to you if you sit down and ask them.

Any time you have a tax bill that comes out of the Senate Finance Committee at two o'clock in the morning, you do have a deadline problem. In 1982 they didn't do anything before six o'clock at night that entire year. The budget itself was late the night of Memorial Day. When the House voted down five budgets, they did it at eleven o'clock at night. You wrote your lead early, and your lead changed. I guess that's what makes editors think Congress is a bunch of idiots—they are not predictable. The White House at least is predictable. But I don't really blame my editors too much, because if you can come up with good stories from Congress, they will find the news interesting.

Where the White House has an effect is a story's play. You'll have a good story from the Congress, but if Reagan says it the next day, that's more important.

In terms of the Senate versus the House, I find the House a much more intelligent group of people to cover because they have rules, because they are more accessible, because they explain things. The Senate really has declined as an institution, in terms of being able to cover it. Its debate is virtually nonexistent. Members come and go from the floor. It is very much a bottom-line institution now, where you cover the vote and don't get much debate. The House in one afternoon will compress the entire issue of the covert action in Nicaragua into a debate, very moving at times and very good.

MR. LINSKY: Jonathan Wolman, what about the wire service perspective?

JONATHAN WOLMAN: I suppose we have the craziest mission of anybody here, covering Congress for national and international news, and also trying to provide regional coverage. We also have some problems with Congress that all the reporters around the table probably share.

The first one is certainly access. It's true that they talk on Capitol Hill, but it's also true that they don't talk on Capitol Hill. Gary Hymel said this morning that you never hear from 365 members of the House, and it's absolutely true. Many of our reporters have probably never heard from hundreds of members of Congress, and there is precious little reporting on what they do day to day. These members issue their press releases to the local papers and, I'm sure, send videotape to the broadcast outlets. But I really doubt whether there is critical—and I mean that in a straightforward sense—coverage of them.

I also think it's difficult for the media to cover decisionmaking on Capitol Hill. Howard Baker [senator, R-Tennessee] is one of the best known and most effective politicians in town—probably considered the most effective politician in Washington right now—but how he makes his decisions is a matter of conjecture to the people who cover him most closely. We don't know who his most influential aides are, or what calls he receives during the day and to what extent he listens to them. It's a process, ironically, that the media pay intense attention to at the White House—and with relatively little success—but less attention to on Capitol Hill.

We don't know what home district pressures the members face. I think the bank withholding story took most reporters absolutely by surprise. Nobody understood where the pressures came from to reverse the provision on banks' withholding interest for taxes.

We get a lot of interest in providing more interpretation, on Capitol Hill as well as elsewhere. But on Capitol Hill it's harder because there are so many diverse reasons why a member might vote a particular way on a bill. And when you focus on the big picture, you often miss the little things that make Congress such a fascinating place. It's very difficult to tell that story.

Peculiar to the wire services, finally, is the question of when to write a story. We used to write about the introduction of every bill, but that got out of hand and went by the wayside. We still pretty much track the subcommittees. The question is, when do readers need the information? I think that's the toughest call we face.

NEWS WITH AN IMPACT ON READERS

CLARK HOYT: I haven't said one word yet and I feel beat up already.

I'm one of those editors out there making decisions which seem to displease both the reporters and the members of Congress. I spent seven years on the Hill covering Congress. I was intensely interested in the folkways, in the process, and in the results. I now have a very different perspective, editing a newspaper half a continent away. I am much less interested in the process. I am interested in final results. I am therefore less interested in Congress as a whole these days, because there seems to be less of that coming out. From my vantage point out there on the Great Plains, if I wanted to apply one word to Congress, it would be "stalemate." Stalemate may be a good Sunday perspective piece once in a while, but it does not make good stories in the rush of day-to-day news.

Reporters whom I control are going to be looking for the news that has immediate impact on my readers. That will tend to be more and more at the White House and at federal agencies.

MR. LINSKY: I want to begin giving people with congressional experience a chance to respond by asking John Culver whether the nature of coverage as described here has any impact on the Congress itself, on the way it performs its duties.

MAKING INFORMATION MORE ACCESSIBLE

JOHN C. CULVER: We start with the fundamental tension between the responsibilities of the members of Congress on the one hand and those of the media on the other. From a congressional point of view, there is a general preoccupation with having their activities presented in the most favorable, positive, popular light, to help ensure their reelection. On the other side, the media have a responsibility to inform the public and seek the truth. So you start with that basic difference.

The other basic difference is that members of Congress, regardless of how anxious they are to be presented in a favorable context, do have to address themselves to the frequently unglamorous slog of the process in the inescapable substantive obligations of their job. As Clark Hoyt just observed, the editors have to sell papers, they have to keep circulation up, they have to address what interests the people. Those, frankly, aren't the same.

Therefore, we get problems. First, the media deal with scandals, superficialities, faux pas, peccadilloes, and the kind of thing that makes human interest news. Second, the media often deal with the problems that reinforce cynicism and negativism—junketing, that sort of thing—things people "understand."

Having said that, it seems to me we do have common problems. One is this complex, decentralized Congress with highly technical issues, many individuals to cover and/or to deal with, many committees, and complex legislative procedures and rules. I have often been impressed with how well, as Dick Fenno says, the media does cover the news. I remember going home at two or three in the morning after one of those sessions and anxiously awaiting Helen Dewar's [*Washington Post*] story to find out what we really did, which amendments were passed and which were defeated, so I could have a clear sense of it and answer my local press inquiries the next day at the office. So, although I share the general congressional frustration with the incessant tendency to reinforce cynicism and negativism about everything we do, I think there is still a remarkable amount of able reporting going on. With all the technical complexity of these issues, I am impressed with how disarmingly many of the major bureau people cover this incredibly complex landscape. These matters are highly technical, and dedicated specialists would be better, but in the real world it's not going to happen.

So what are we going to do to improve the system? One change we might consider would be to develop opportunities for the media to have access to information concerning the background of substantive issues as well as the rules and procedures that are decisive. Some direction and briefing may also be needed on key players—not just the familiar media faces that everybody comes back to, but the people who are really making it work. Some instruction and direction might be provided through computer technology, to make retrievals of historical precedent, and so forth, instantaneously available.

I know the Senate Democrats have opened a press office since I left the Senate. Representatives of the Democratic and Republican Policy Committees in the Senate could have weekly briefings to discuss what's coming up. The parliamentarian and his assistant could be there to talk about rules or procedural problems, and the resources of the Congressional Library could be used for retrieval capabilities on breaking issues. And these think tanks in Washington could be organized to have timely, topical briefing sessions for all these bureaus, particularly the ones that don't have the more sophisticated capability.

The other major point where we've got a vacuum is home-state reporting. We oscillate. We either cover the big issues too much—everybody runs to where the cameras are, the sexy current thing going on—or we cover all the trivial scandals excessively. What drops between the cracks is most of the work of the Congress. You don't have much substantive regional reporting about members from various delegations. We have a good bureau from the *Des Moines Register*. It does a remarkable job. But in most of the regional press, even those that have stringers, the coverage is all human interest.

Related to that is one of the biggest problems that has gone unmentioned here: senators and congressmen who go back home to run, particularly senators running every six years, have a terribly tough time communicating effectively with their local press on issues involving Congress. Back in the state you live or die for reelection. How are the media going to equip the local political editors to ask the right questions, to bring out the scorekeeping kind of information? Maybe state media groups should sponsor seminars, or maybe using technology they can do more, because nothing is more frustrating than trying to penetrate that ignorance. You have to filter information through that ignorance to reach the people, and that's a very serious media breakdown.

MR. LINSKY: Let's assume for the moment that the press isn't going to deal with that problem. Is there anything that Congress can do, members individually or the Congress institutionally?

MR. CULVER: What Barber Conable did made excellent sense. We used to do that. We would have these local area breakfasts every time we ran, every two years. You had these terrible issues like a balanced budget, and it would come out "Culver against a balanced budget, so-and-so for a balanced budget." Well, it's a little more complicated than that. We tried to set aside an hour to sit down informally, respond, and give some handouts, in an effort to educate.

I think the member has that kind of obligation and responsibility, but we need a lot of help. Something that would really help would be for state broadcast and print organizations to send their abler young political reporters to find out what Congress is all about. The media has a responsibility, totally independent of the congressional one, to enhance its capabilities in that regard.

MR. LINSKY: Peter Teeley, is there anything that the Congress can do to deal with the way the institution and the activities are perceived back home?

AN INDIVIDUAL RESPONSE

PETER F. TEELEY: As an institution it's very tough, because you have so many people with different opinions. My suggestion is that members of Congress take a look at their own, individual operations and try to start from there. If you are dealing with the War Powers Act, for example, before enactment bring in a couple of wire service reporters, the *New York Times*, the *Washington Post*, the *Los Angeles Times*, the three newsmagazines, and the networks. Have a series of meetings to talk about the legislative process, the way the legislation is moving, the pros and cons. Then you are essentially covering the major media outlets in this country, those institutions that shape and form perceptions. If you do this over a period of months, people will know that issue inside out. They will know your strengths and your vulnerabilities on the issue. But let's face it: A lot of members are afraid of the press. They don't want to speak to reporters; they would just as soon get in, vote, and get out.

I'd just like to say one thing about what John Culver mentioned—briefings to provide information to reporters. That should be attempted. However, because of the various factions in the two political parties, it's going to be very difficult to have a unified position on an issue. Let's take one example, the Kemp-Roth tax bill which was basically picked up by the administration and adopted by the Congress. While people like Barber Conable and Bob Dole and others voted for it, they had serious reservations. It would be hard to bring them together in a unified march and say, look, here's our position, here are our statistics, this is what we agree on. I don't think you're going to have that. You have to look back to the individual office and try to do it there.

MR. ROGERS: I don't think you want—I don't think anyone in the press wants—Congress to package. One of the advantages of Congress is that it is the best reflection, as an institution, of the country. The fact that Barber Conable and Bob Dole were uncomfortable with aspects of the Kemp-Roth bill was fundamental to the story. It reflects a White House mentality to want to get everything together. What you cover Congress for is not to have everything together.

MR. CULVER: Could I clarify one point? The substantive presentation of competing arguments for and against particular issues is best done under a forum like a think-tank program. What I'm talking about is briefings about rules and procedures and that kind of thing, from the parliamentarian's office, totally neutral. That could give insight and direction. It could direct reporters' inquiries and save time for more substantive development of the issues. Also, it would help in terms of having some kind of identification of key staff and players in a particular debate.

THE DEMISE OF CLEARCUT ISSUES

HARRY McPHERSON: At least half the discussion so far this morning was encapsulated for me many years ago in the Oval Office, when Lyndon Johnson and Henry Luce [founder and editor, *Time*] were having a conversation. I happened to be in the room. Johnson was waving *Time* in front of Luce. He said, "Look at this. This week 200,000 blacks registered in the South, thanks to the Voting Rights Act. Three hundred thousand elderly people are going to be covered by Medicare. We have a hundred thousand young unemployed kids working in neighborhoods. Is any of that in there? No. What's in here?" And there followed some rather scatological language about what was in there, Vietnam and riots and stuff like that. He said, "Where's the other stuff?" And Luce looked at him very sadly, and shook his head and said, "Mr. President, good news isn't news. Bad news is news." That's the essential conflict that John Culver was talking about. News isn't the slow movement of the buses taking another hundred thousand students to Job Corps camps; it's the riot in the street that is both photogenic and easier to cover.

You asked originally about the problems that the press has. One is simply issues. In my years in Washington, issues have gone from relatively simple white hat-black hat issues, to more complex ones where there is less agreement.

It used to be that you could send out a bunch of reporters and maybe even a television camera when Judge Howard K. Smith [former member of Congress, D-Virginia] was the head of the Rules Committee. Is Judge Smith going to let the little black children do this, or is he going to go out fishing and turn his back on the liberal wishes of the people? It was part of the process, but it was also black-white. It was really head-on confrontation: civil rights or no civil rights. It was both photogenic and "newsgenic"—I mean, you could write it as well as photograph it.

What about today? What's the effect of this gigantic deficit? Clark Hoyt says out there in Wichita he doesn't want to have a bunch of long process articles; he wants things that will have an impact on the reader. But the deficit is going to have an impact on the reader one of these days. It's a big fight. Within the administration, the chairman of the Council of Economic Advisers says one thing and the Treasury Department says something quite different. Where is Congress? How would you cover that issue to have an impact on television?

MR. LINSKY: Is that a problem for Congress or for the press?

MR. McPHERSON: Jackie Adams just asked how you get all that in a minute and a half. I don't think you do. You have to persuade the networks to do what they used to do. It's within the memory of living men that the networks used to devote some time, maybe two hours, to a hearing that wasn't about somebody getting caught in some page's bedroom. You could watch the Foreign Relations Committee on the Vietnam War, with [Dean] Rusk [former Secretary of State] up there testifying. They don't do stuff like that any more. It seems to me network news is getting softer and more like Mr. [Rupert] Murdoch [publisher, *New York Post*]. And it will ultimately get that way almost totally.

Anyway, I want to endorse what John Culver recommended. I was thinking about the utility of some of the main committees at least—the Energy and Commerce Committee in the House, Finance Committee, Ways and Means Committee, maybe Foreign Affairs and Foreign Relations Committee—having press secretaries. Maybe you have to have two press secretaries, one for each party, to describe what's going on.

MR. WOLMAN: The staff will never tell the press secretary what's happening.

MR. McPHERSON: The best press knows how to go to the staff,

but what about the small bureaus that are hard-pressed and don't have time to cover all the hearings at Energy and Commerce? What about having a press office for them, or a daily briefing to talk about what the committee has been doing?

MR. HUNT: One thing there's no shortage of in the Congress is access. I hate to disagree with you, but I really do. We don't have a problem getting to see people.

DIFFERENT MEDIA, DIFFERENT MISSIONS

NORMAN J. ORNSTEIN: Let me bring the focus back to media problems with Congress and to your first question, the mission. It seems to me we missed something here: There are different missions, and they change over time.

Start with national television. We talked mostly about the nightly news, but it seems to me that the whole mission of television is changing. Nightly news is in many respects diminishing in importance and in audience. But we have seen a dramatic change in what television is doing elsewhere: an hour-long *MacNeil-Lehrer* show, *Nightline*, C-SPAN, *This Week With David Brinkley* and now *Face the Nation* changing to meet that. Their goals and the needs are very different from those of the nightly news.

Newspapers are changing too, both in the local and national face. National newspapers, journals, and a lot of newsletters have no problems with Congress, and Congress has almost no problems with them. David Rogers wrote a story a couple of years ago on a fight for a committee assignment on the Ways and Means Committee, about as inside-baseball as you could get. Fascinating, and I think something that could hit home to local readers. He didn't have a problem getting it prominent coverage in the *Boston Globe*.

Television would have a different set of problems. A profile of Jamie Whitten [member of Congress, D-Mississippi] back in his district and in Washington, which would be very nice to do, will never run on the evening news. But you might convince Charles Kuralt to run it on *Sunday Morning*, and it would get a substantial audience.

We have seen the number of newspapers diminish dramatically, as well as change in their mission. The *Minneapolis Tribune and Star* partly because the revenues have diminished, no longer cares about coverage of Congress or coverage of anything significant in politics. In many respects, local newspapers like that are a lost cause. They aren't going to pay attention to anything that we say because their bottom line changed. They have less ad space and less of a news hole.

Chains are taking over a lot of these local newspapers, and a chain like Cowles may not pay much attention to news. Other chains do—Knight-Ridder, for example; the *St. Paul Pioneer Press* gives much better coverage to Congress than the Minneapolis papers. Congress might become a little more sensitive to those people who run the chains. If members of Congress spent a little more time with Allen Neuharth [chairman, Gannett Newspapers], it might not change his coldhearted view of the bottom line, but it might influence Gannett a little bit to cover some of these stories. If more time were spent with the wire services, which have become an even more dominant source of news for these kinds of papers as their mission has changed, we might well see a different focus.

One last thing. There's another disturbing trend in television: Local television affiliates are having more control over what goes out on the network news. They don't care, as local newspapers don't, about any of this kind of stuff, and they are exerting pressure that might change the focus in the wrong fashion.

THE PRESS'S RESPONSIBILITY

MR. RENNERT: I'd like to dissent a bit from what has been said. My impression is that in the last ten years the trend has been positive, though perhaps with some exceptions. We not only have more regional correspondents on the Hill, but I think we have better trained, more capable people writing better stuff.

We discussed earlier the problem of individual scorekeeping. When I was doing regional reporting I did umpteen stories about the California delegation, both collectively and individually, to point out who were the top people in the delegation, why they were the top people, who were the secondary and tertiary players, and how the delegation as a whole functioned—usually not well. It was always, I thought, a good story because it was the biggest delegation on the Hill and yet it was fairly weak.

I talked earlier about this underlying cynicism on both sides of the fence. My own sense, having been in Washington almost twenty years, is that one of the remedies is for the press to give equal attention to the individuals on the Hill who really do a superior job and who very often are totally inaccessible. Phil Burton [former member of Congress, D-California] was a classic example. He had his door closed to the press; he would not communicate because he was making his private deals. He was being very effective, and to me it was a challenge to penetrate and see how he operated and what he accomplished, instead of concentrating on the sizzle. That was what most other people were writing: Here is this overbearing, arrogant so-and-so, a loudmouth who arm-twists. The stories I liked to do about Phil Burton were how he got Jamie Whitten and Otto Passman [former member of Congress, D-Louisiana] to support him in getting black lung through by making a deal with the King Cotton people in the South.

So the stories are there. I dissent from John Culver's view that you'll improve the situation a lot by giving us more briefings. That would result in a marginal improvement. Greater improvement has to come from the press, the people the editors send here, their mission, and what the editors are going to use.

One postscript—and I'm sort of biting the hand that feeds us today. The people at the *Los Angeles Times* know I've been critical of their coverage of the California delegation. They have great national and international coverage, but when you talk about individual scorekeeping, how individual members perform on the Hill and how the legislation that they really care about is moving, they can, in my view, do a much better job.

MR. LINSKY: Bill Cable, is there any room for an institutional response or an individual response by members of the Congress?

WILLIAM H. CABLE: There's room for individual responses. The biggest problem with an institutional response is that there isn't an institution. It is a House, it is a Senate. It is a John Dingell [member of Congress, D-Michigan] at the Energy Committee, it was a Phil Burton.

The Democratic leadership in the House has tried to institutionalize a response over the last several years by having a fifteen-minute press conference each day. That's used pretty much as an agenda-setting process for the House for the day—at least it was for the four years I watched from the White House end—and it seems to work well.

The frustration is one of members, particularly in the House, afraid to deal with the press. That's something that they have to do individually. Barber Conable's example of bringing in and getting comfortable with his folks at home is the only way any member is going to have that kind of relationship. You have to take a chance, basically, that they are not out to write the worst story. If you don't have that relationship, you'll never have an opportunity to give your side to the people who write.

MR. LINSKY: Chuck Jones, pick up on the institutional approaches for improving coverage.

IT OUGHT TO BE DIFFICULT

MR. JONES: First of all, I want to say I glory in the difficulties the press has in covering Congress. It's relatively easy to cover the House of Commons, and you can cover the Supreme Soviet from here. But it's difficult to cover Congress for very good reasons. If Congress is doing its job, it isn't going to be easy to cover because it's going to happen in lots of different places, in offices, in committees and subcommittees, and on the floor. I couldn't be happier about that.

Before any kind of analysis of the media's role, we have to ask a couple of questions. What is it we want people to know about Congress? And, can they find out?

Television is so different it deserves different treatment, not necessarily by the standards of print journalism. My guess is that we are just in the process of trying to figure out what standards to apply to that new thing, the pictures with talk. It hasn't been worked out yet. What does it do? What does it do well? Are there some ways to improve it?

The variety of print media perform most of the functions we want, but no one does it all. I'm not worried, in part because both sides are so worried. There are lots of sources available.

MR. DUKE: May I enter a dissenting voice about this whole question of gathering information? It's been suggested that it is difficult to cover Congress. I happen to feel that it is not really that difficult.

Sure, there's a lot going on every day on the Hill, and a lot of it is complex and complicated. To find out what's going on, a reporter really has to dig, and he has to be on the run a lot of the time. He has to have a feel for the legislative process and for politics in general, and he has to be reasonably intelligent.

But, having said that, I do not think it is true that the staff never tells the press what's going on. In my experience on the Hill I have found staff people quite cooperative, quite willing to help the press understand and get the facts straight. Any reporter worth his salt can find out what's going on on the Hill. Maybe not everything. Maybe it takes time. It certainly requires a little digging. But you can find out. The process is a lot more open now.

MR. LINSKY: That's an interesting point, because we really are talking about two different Congresses. We are talking about the one that members who use initiative display, and we are talking about the one that David Rogers's or Al Hunt's long take-out or a documentary can show.

MICHAEL J. ROBINSON: When Margaret Sheehan and I did the research for *Over the Wire and on TV*, we looked at presidential and congressional news coverage in 1940, 1960, and 1980. What we found is that the coverage of Congress today is not wrong, it's not dumb, it's not ideologically biased, it does not focus on showhorses. Mike Barnes [member of Congress, D-Maryland] may be a showhorse, but he's also the subcommittee chairman on Latin American Affairs; he's the one who appears on the news. We also found congressional coverage to be fairly broad. Compared with 1940 we have longer coverage and better coverage and broader coverage.

So I find it hard to understand Congress's complaint. Members still get reelected generally, and more laws are passed decade by decade. I don't see a problem with people not understanding what's going on in Congress more than in the past. I don't see people deciding not to obey Congress because what they see on television is generally negative.

I do have some difficulties with television and press coverage of Congress as an institution. Phil Jones of CBS inevitably defines trips home to the district as vacations where members are blowing off time. I don't think that's accurate. It is true that the press has always looked at what is negative, not what is positive. That's a problem. But these are not altogether terrible problems, and they are problems of democracy. Over the last forty years, both have done a better job—Congress with what it does and the press with what it does.

A PROBLEM OF DEMOCRACY

MR. EHRENHALT: It seems to me that about half of us are talking about supply and the others are talking about demand.

The supply issue is: Does Congress make its information accessible enough? Are reporters willing to provide the information to their editors and readers? Are members of Congress accessible enough? There is an ample supply of this information. In one sense members of Congress and reporters are on the same side. Members want to communicate information, and reporters, in my experience, want to provide it.

The real problem is: Is there a demand at the newspaper level and the local television level, and among the readers and listeners? I think that's what we ought to focus on. The institutional changes we are talking about might make sense, but they won't do much to solve that problem. I'm not sure anything would.

We are talking about a problem of democracy. Most people, most of the time, are not interested in Congress as an institution. It doesn't make any difference how much access we get to members of Congress. It doesn't make much difference how many seminars Congress holds for us.

MR. CULVER: The important thing that seems missing here is differentiation. We talked about apples and oranges, or television and the print media. We ought to be specific. The same is true when you go to people. Al Hunt or Johnny Apple [*New York Times*] or David Rogers has a very sophisticated, long experience with that institution. Of course it's not hard for them. Tip O'Neill, Ted Kennedy, anybody will break legs getting to the phone in most cases when they call.

What I really had in mind was these places that can't afford a significant presence in Washington. They use stringers, who most of the time are very inexperienced and have no resources. They could use some help to perform the responsibility that some guy back home is insisting they perform. We can talk forever about problems, but some specific recommendations have to be addressed.

MR. LINSKY: Clark Hoyt and Alan Ehrenhalt said readers don't want that stuff, so it's Congress's problem.

MR. HOYT: Our readers want to read that stuff in the broadest sense, which means news about things that affect them. Kansas is physically remote in this country. It has four main ingredients to its economy: the petroleum industry, aviation manufacturing, cattle, and wheat. Every one of those things is dependent on what happens in Washington, and also on what happens in Saudi Arabia or around the world. Our readers care a lot. They are sophisticated. We spend a lot of resources trying to bring information to them. When you are sifting through all of this to fill a finite news hole, though, you come down to a decision about which is of most immediate importance. On a day-to-day basis, the process of Congress does get lost because it does not have an impact.

TELEVISION THE OPINION-MAKER

MR. CABLE: Most of the people in this country get most of their news in Jackie's minute-and-a-half clips. That's something that needs to be said. That's the frustration Dave Obey feels, getting slammed by Harry Reasoner in an unconscionable way, though that's not a minute and a half. That's a problem that we can't address in terms of access, or who gets what kind of information, or who gets what kind of briefings. And that problem is magnified, because that minute-and-a-half spot has an inordinate influence on public opinion, which is what makes a lot of the guys on the Hill tick. That is the nature of the problem.

I don't know how you solve that. I don't think you're going to solve it by picking which piece of the Pentagon's report you're going to write up for the airplane manufacturers, or whether the mining of the harbor between the Iraqis and the Iranians is good news or bad news for the petroleum industry. That minute and a half is where the opinion is made, where it affects Congress's or the President's ability to deliver.

MR. ROGERS: That comes through in this discussion because the members talk the networks and about local coverage. You don't really give a damn about what the *Boston Globe* does unless you live in Massachusetts, and you don't really care that much about the *Post* except as the *Post* influences the networks.

MR. CULVER: In Iowa—which has the highest literacy rate—every one of our polls shows the public gets news from television. The *Des Moines Register* is unique, it's on everyone's doorstep every day, and it's highly respected, but it can't compete in terms of where they get their news.

MR. HUNT: It strikes me that one of the great advantages of the Congress is that it's probably the best place in government to cover important issues. You can cover what's going on in taxes much better from Capitol Hill than you can from the Treasury. You can certainly cover the defense budget much better on Capitol Hill than you can from the Pentagon. Some of these stories are difficult, they're complex, they're probably dull, and it's up to us to figure out ways to make them more interesting. It doesn't do any good to do an important piece if nobody watches it or nobody reads it.

THREE AUDIENCES

MR. ORNSTEIN: To be simplistic, I think we can talk about three categories of audience. Each has different needs.

There is an elite of elites, two or three or five percent of the public who read the *Wall Street Journal*, who perhaps read *Congressional Quarterly*, who at least read the congressional news stories. We don't have to worry about them; they will find what they want.

There's another elite of perhaps twenty percent who watch the evening news and from time to time watch C-SPAN. They'll perhaps watch *MacNeil-Lehrer*, they might watch *Sunday Morning*, they may pay attention to other media. We ought to pay some attention to how we can improve their understanding. That's in a different fashion; it's not necessarily just the minute and a half on evening news.

When it comes to a broader public, I suspect there's almost nothing that can be done, except perhaps to find better ways to jawbone the evening news so that the minute and twenty seconds doesn't deal with vague allegations about who might have had sex with a page, and move toward more substance.

MR. RENNERT: I would like to inject a note of caution against rushing pell-mell toward institutional reforms to help out what some here perceive as a problem of access. I don't think access is a great problem, even for regional bureaus.

I would also like to point out something that hasn't been mentioned yet. We have seen this great trend toward bureaucratization on the Hill, particularly on the Senate side, in recent years. And, as you develop more institutional facilities with the best of intentions to help either members of Congress or reporters, I think you'll get counterproductive results.

I would fire ninety percent of the press secretaries on the Hill. If members are really interested in good access and good relations with the press, nine times out of ten the press secretary is an impediment, somebody trying to create images. It's make-work. This goes for a lot of other staff too. The important staff are the legislative aides, the technicians, who ought to be easily accessible. The members, particularly on the Senate side, also ought to be more accessible. By reducing staff you would help more than by creating new staff.

MR. WOLMAN: It's key not to add another layer, be it think tank or press secretary.

MR. ROBINSON: I speak to civil servants in the District of Columbia about forty times a year. A majority of them do not know who the Majority Leader is in the Senate. At least two-thirds don't know who the Majority Leader is in the House. The press is at least telling them that. The press and Congress should understand that if the public doesn't know something, it isn't necessarily because the networks or the print press aren't telling them. I think that is every bit as important as anything else that we can say here.

MR. LINSKY: Harry McPherson, can you tie this all together?

THE PROBLEM OF MANY VOICES

MR. McPHERSON: I sure can't.

Nobody wants to go back to the days of control by a few people, but Congress has become so proliferated that it puts itself at an increasing disadvantage in getting coverage. When one person speaks for the executive branch, it's the president. Therefore, the press can stand in front of the White House every night and say that the executive branch of the government—that means everybody from the Defense Department, State, Interior, Consumer Products Safety Commission—is speaking through this fellow.

Go out on the Hill, where is it? All over the lot. This is something that Congress really ought to address. It has created a problem as it has distributed influence and power and staff. Congress really needs to think in press relations terms if it's going to deal with one voice on the Hill. It's got to be able to make a fist when it responds.

MR. JONES: May I close by saying I couldn't disagree more.

5

THE INGREDIENTS OF CONGRESSIONAL NEWS
A Case Discussion

PARTICIPANTS

Joseph L. Bower (moderator), professor of business administration, Harvard Business School; author, *The Two Faces of Management: An American Approach to Leadership in Business and Government*

Jacqueline Adams, Capitol Hill correspondent, CBS News

Paul Duke, moderator, *Washington Week in Review*

Alan Ehrenhalt, political editor, *Congressional Quarterly*

Charles D. Ferris, attorney, Mintz, Levin, Cohn, Ferris, Glovsky and Popeo; former general counsel, Senate Democratic Policy Committee; former chairman, Federal Communications Commission

Bill Frenzel, member of Congress, R-Minnesota

Paul Houston, congressional correspondent, *Los Angeles Times*

Clark Hoyt, managing editor, *Wichita Eagle-Beacon*

Gary Hymel, executive vice president, Gray & Co.; former press secretary to Speaker of the House Thomas P. (Tip) O'Neill (D-Massachusetts)

James McCartney, national correspondent, Knight-Ridder Newspapers

Harry McPherson, partner, Verner, Lipfert, Bernhard & McPherson: former assistant counsel to the Senate Democratic Policy Committee; former special counsel to President Johnson

Norman J. Ornstein, visiting scholar, American Enterprise Institute; editor, *Congress in Change*

James B. Pearson, former senator, R-Kansas

Leo Rennert, Washington bureau chief, McClatchy Newspapers of California

Michael J. Robinson, associate professor of government, Georgetown University; author (with Margaret A. Sheehan), *Over the Wire and On TV: CBS and UPI in Campaign '80*

Peter E. Teeley, press secretary to Vice-President George Bush (on leave); Fellow, Institute of Politics, Harvard University

INTRODUCTORY NOTE:

As a starting point for the discussion, the following hypothetical case, prepared by Stephen Bates, was distributed in advance:

A successful and popular drug rehabilitation center, located on an isolated site on federal land, is destroyed by fire. The state's senior senator, Jefferson Smith, introduces a bill to rebuild the center with federal funds. Smith, who is chairman of the committee to which the bill is referred, and his staff work closely with a Washington lobbyist, Longfellow Deeds, who is volunteering his services. Deeds arranges for a popular rock singer named Norman Maine to testify in favor of the bill.

A week later, the lobbyist, Deeds, tips off a reporter that a major oil company has been trying to get the Secretary of the Interior to release the land for drilling. The company has hired an influential lobbyist named Floyd Thursby to work against the Smith bill. The reporter also hears a rumor that Senator Seab Cooley, who is leading the opposition to rebuilding the center, has received a $5,000 contribution from the oil company's PAC.

The day before the committee vote, the oil company lobbyist, Thursby, calls the reporter. Thursby claims that Deeds, the lobbyist who has been helping Smith, is employed by the Saudi government and that the Saudis want the center rebuilt so that the oil deposits in the region will remain untapped. The reporter goes to Deeds for confirmation. Deeds admits that the Saudis have retained his lobbying firm. But he insists that he has never worked on their account, and that the work he is doing for the Smith bill is pro bono.

JOSEPH L. BOWER: Should Norman Maine's testimony be covered? Why or why not?

STAR-STUDDED HEARINGS

BILL FRENZEL: I don't think there's any good reason, but based on experience I assume that's the headline for the whole story. It will get more inches or more time simply because he's a Joan Baez or a Robert Redford.

MR. BOWER: A celebrity can always get the news?

MR. FRENZEL: No question about it.

NORMAN J. ORNSTEIN: It wouldn't be big news in the newspapers, but you would find it on the evening news because you're talking about stars. In many instances they have become stars on a screen somewhere, and now the television screen shows that. So Brooke Shields is shown when she testifies against smoking, and Walter Cronkite is shown when he testifies for Senate television—which weren't stories in the newspapers. There has really been a tremendous increase in these things. You find celebrities in Washington more often than in Hollywood.

JACQUELINE ADAMS: I'm not sure that Mr. Maine would get on the evening news. He might get on radio, and he might get on the morning news. If it were a real slow day, maybe he would get on the evening news.

MR. ORNSTEIN: Brooke Shields made all three evening news shows when she came to testify, in a situation where there wasn't even a bill.

LEO RENNERT: It strikes me that the events of the first week—their Senator introducing the bill—are very productive for the home-state papers, particularly the paper in the community where the camp burned down. If you had a hearing on this kind of a bill, whether a Norman Maine testified or not, we would cover it. If he did testify, we might give him a few paragraphs, but we would not ignore the mayor or the governor or the director of the drug rehabilitation center who came too. It's not big national news or television news, but it certainly is big home-town news.

GARY HYMEL: We spend too much time kicking hell out of television news for what it covers; we should point out that this is a case where Congress manipulates television. The only reason they have that guy there is to sucker in the television press.

CLARK HOYT: I would be unlikely to run the hearing as a breaking story, but I might wind up using Norman Maine as a way to get into a story about the bill and who is for it, who is against it, and why.

MR. BOWER: So in one case the celebrity is the story: in another case the celebrity is the peg for the story.

PAROCHIAL STORIES THAT BECOME NATIONAL

PETER E. TEELEY: In the early stages it isn't really much of a story. It is important to Leo Rennert's area, but it really doesn't become any kind of a national story until they find out they have three billion barrels of oil underneath. If it's only twenty-five thousand barrels, nobody is going to get too excited.

MR. BOWER: You're saying the first thing the reporter needs to do is find out how much oil is underneath?

MR. TEELEY: I think so. There would be a hell of a difference in the way they treat a story once they find the amount of oil.

JAMES McCARTNEY: I agree that it's basically a regional story, not a national story. The attention Norman Maine might get would depend, at least to me, on the quality and the relevance of his testimony. At this point I might give it two paragraphs on an inside page.

PAUL HOUSTON: This might be a major story, if it were in the context of a Jim Watt [former Secretary of the Interior] and development versus protection. Depending on how much oil was there, and in the context of a broader pattern of development of public lands, this could be major.

MR. BOWER: If you want to play the story at this stage, how do you do it?

MR. RENNERT: On what we call the local section page. It's not a page-one story, even in the home-town paper.

JAMES B. PEARSON: So far as the Senate would be concerned, it would be a very parochial issue and it would be treated as a parochial issue. And, if Congress treats an issue as parochial, the press tends to treat it as parochial too.

MR. BOWER: If you were Senator Cooley, you saw this thing coming at you, and you opposed it for any reason, would you feel it was important to get your side of the story covered?

MR. PEARSON: I'm not sure I would. If I'm opposing a parochial bill to rebuild a rehabilitation facility—something a lot of people would view as interesting and vital—I don't want a lot of publicity.

MR. ORNSTEIN: It's worth noting that a parochial story can become a national story under several sets of circumstances. We have just seen one. There was a little parochial story about a handful of elderly families in Oregon. The question was whether the land that they had purchased thirty-five or forty years ago was in fact public land; the Interior Department was trying to make them pay a very large amount of money. That remained a parochial story, mostly out of the public focus, until Jim Watt persuaded Ronald Reagan to veto the bill that gave them redress. Then it became a major national story. National actors make a national story. Another set of circumstances is when some celebrity gets dragged in on an issue that otherwise wouldn't be well noticed. The third set is if there's a scandal involved. If you found a parochial issue in which a member was taking a bribe, that would become national.

MR. BOWER: Then you can use a celebrity to take a small story and give it national coverage.

MR. ORNSTEIN: Television coverage.

USING TELEVISION TO GET PRINT COVERAGE

MR. RENNERT: Not only television. Editors back home see the news and they want stories to match. I'm not the only one; I hear this from many colleagues in the print media. And it's not only celebrities, but also other things that television does. So we in the print media should not be holier than thou about it. Unfortunately, you can hire Norman Maine, get his puss on television, and through TV also force newspaper correspondents. You can manipulate beyond television.

MS. ADAMS: It's not just network television, either. There's a tremendous proliferation of local and regional television coverage as well. Just because there's a bill and a rock star, I doubt CBS will go. But you can be sure representatives of all the television stations in that area are going to be there, and that might be how your editor would learn about it.

MR. BOWER: If it was really dead on a Sunday night, with nothing having happened over the weekend, would that increase the likelihood of your using it nationally?

PAUL DUKE: Television news is increasingly more sophisticated than that. In Washington we call these "dog and pony shows," and we have seen a lot of them before Congress in recent years. It has almost reached the point where there is a diminishing return. Television news producers are more aware when somebody is seeking publicity and in reality there's no news.

MICHAEL J. ROBINSON: Back during the Korean War, the Republicans were delighted to give Douglas MacArthur an opportunity to come on and speak against Harry Truman. The biggest change is not so much that the networks are covering hearings and print isn't; they both cover hearings. The big change is that in 1950 it was Douglas MacArthur, but in 1980 it was more likely to be Jackson Brown or Rick Springfield. I couldn't say that's an effect of television news, though. Media celebrities are becoming more important in the entire political realm.

WHEN TO AVOID PUBLICITY

MR. BOWER: This isn't the tax reform bill; it's a modest piece of legislation. How important are coverage and public awareness to get momentum?

CHARLES D. FERRIS: That goes to a basic question. This is a type of issue where you don't go through the classic process of putting in a bill, having hearings, marking it up, and sending it over. This is one where you go to the Appropriations Committee chairman and ask him to take care of this project in your district. And he takes care of it. Senator Smith must have made the judgment that Senator Cooley would beat him in the cloakroom, so he had to go the high-visibility route—putting in the bill and trying to get publicity. That takes much longer, and it is a higher-risk venture, than the backroom process.

MR. FRENZEL: In the real world you don't have hearings. No Senate committee chairman would ever be denied the building of a thing like this. We had one last year when Senator Pete Domenici [R-New Mexico] wanted to block the imports of uranium. That was considered Pete's deal; the Senate gave it to him a thousand to nothing, even though it had important international and national policy implications. So we would never hear about this.

MR. BOWER: This would be a courtesy issue, in effect.

MR. PEARSON: If I was handling it, I'd put it in and move it out of committee the first time we had any mark-ups on anything. If I did anything in the way of press relations I'd send a little notice back home.

MR. BOWER: Nonetheless, we know there are instances where Senators do run elaborate hearings in order to create a record. We tracked the whole deregulation of the airlines, [Edward M.] Kennedy's [senator, D-Massachusetts] staff in effect scripting a very elaborate set of hearings to do just this sort of thing. So it must happen some of the time.

What we are saying, though, is that there is a whole category of activity which goes unreported, basically because it's a matter of congressional courtesy. And, therefore, Congress can make a great deal of law in private, and the press will basically leave it alone.

MR. FRENZEL: Won't know about it.

MR. RENNERT: Or care.

MR. HYMEL: Press courtesy.

MR. BOWER: So if I have something that I think is the least bit controversial, I'll try to do it through my representatives in the quietest way possible.

Let's move beyond the hearing. Thursby is hired by an oil company, and there is allegedly oil underneath—let's say a fair amount. Do those facts make it a story?

MR. FRENZEL: Yes.

MR. BOWER: What do you do about it?

MR. McCARTNEY: You can't do anything with what you have here. What you have here is rumors. A lot more work has to be done to document it.

MR. BOWER: You call Senator Cooley and Thursby. They won't talk to you. What do you do?

MR. McCARTNEY: You want to find out if there is really oil there, if Cooley really got the money, and if you can document that.

MR. RENNERT: If it's federal land, you call Geological Survey. That's one possibility. There are state agencies, state geologists, too.

MR. BOWER: You're saying that there is still no story until you know how much oil there is. Let me stipulate that you have a hard time finding out, because that tends to be the case. One thing that the Department of Energy doesn't know is where the oil is and how much there is; the oil companies are very uncooperative on that.

MR. DUKE: I think it has become a story of political intrigue the moment you learn that somebody is going to fight it, that Senator Cooley will lead opposition. The reporter has to try to find out what's behind that.

MR. BOWER: Then the things that would make it a story aren't the substance, unless it's big oil or something, but the process.

MR. ROBINSON: If you suspect dark forces, that's a watchdog function, not sensationalism or titillation.

MR. BOWER: Why is the interest of the oil company in a piece of land, and their willingness to work with a senator, a watchdog function—isn't that democracy at work? What's wrong with that?

REPORTING CAMPAIGN CONTRIBUTIONS

MR. HOYT: One thing that would be wrong is if the $5,000 is a quid pro quo.

MR. McCARTNEY: To write a newspaper story about it, you don't have to make a judgment on whether it's right or wrong. You only have to have a conflict between two interests.

MR. BOWER: Let's say it was a big oil PAC contribution to Senator Cooley. What do you need to know before you write the story? Do you need to know all his sources of funds?

MR. McCARTNEY: No.

MR. BOWER: If you just say that Cooley takes money from the oil company, isn't there a clear implication that he's been bought?

MR. McCARTNEY: Might be.

MR. DUKE: One of the things that must be reported here is the total contribution from PACs. If the guy got $600,000 from PACs—I think one member of Congress in 1982 got something like 240 PAC contributions—that helps to put it in perspective. The $5,000 wouldn't seem all that great.

MR. ORNSTEIN: But there are a lot of stories that impute sinister motives to members of Congress for $5,000 or $10,000 combination contributions. You don't have to get to the half-million-dollar level before you see stories written.

ALAN EHRENHALT: While there are stories written about the influence of campaign contributions on members, they are stories about the aggregate. The Banking Committee received so many contributions from banks, for example. The fact that an individual member receives a PAC contribution from somebody with an interest in legislation he's working on simply is not a story. There has to be something fairly close to a quid pro quo, or all of us, with the possible exception of a regional reporter, would simply ignore it. This is the way Congress works, and it isn't news.

MR. RENNERT: I disagree if you bring it up to a high enough factual level. Let's say in the last six months he's gotten twenty oil PAC contributions up to $100,000, and it's a Permian Basin kind of resource. Then, with the juxtaposition of the do-good effort on drug rehabilitation with the oil industry's financial and lobbying muscle on the Hill, it has the makings of a good regional story as well as a national story.

MR. BOWER: What is the story now?

MR. McCARTNEY: You don't have enough even to assign the guy. I wouldn't put anybody on this.

MR. ROBINSON: You're really speaking about investigative journalism, and most congressional coverage is anything but investigative journalism.

HARRY McPHERSON: Almost no paper in the country would print: "Senator Cooley, who has received $5,000 in oil PAC contributions this year, is seeking to fight the bill so the land can be turned over to the oil company for drilling." Maybe three months from now somebody will do a big story about oil company PAC contributions, and that's where it will appear. But you don't interject this parenthetic innuendo that the guy's been bought.

MR. HOYT: You would be irresponsible to print much of what we have at this stage of the process.

MR. BOWER: What I hear is that it's not even a story at this point. You wouldn't allocate investigative time to go after it. It's a small piece of evidence in a pattern story, or it's not on the screen at all.

CONFLICT AS NEWS

MR. HOUSTON: We may have more here than we think. We are worried about the amount of oil. The oil company has been trying to get the Secretary of Interior to release the land for drilling, which implies that there is a lot of oil there. We can find out from two sources, the oil company and the Secretary of the Interior.

We also have four sets of conflicts in the case that indicate a potential story. One conflict is the chairman of a committee, who has a bill for his home state, being fought by another Senator. That's pretty unusual. Number two, you have the land-use conflict, the oil company trying to take over a piece of land that's been used for a popular drug rehabilitation center. That's an interesting conflict. You've also got a PAC contribution involved, a conflict of interest which with further investigation might turn out to be getting into the fringes of bribery, especially with the other facts. The fourth conflict, which we haven't gotten to, is the Saudi government's involvement with a lobbyist on the other side of the issue. You have a possible conflict of interest there. So you have four conflicts. You can get a story out of that.

MR. ORNSTEIN: It depends on the level of conflict. For example, it is now a story if a member's spouse takes a job with an organization on which that member is going to vote. Norman Lent's [member of Congress, R-New York] wife was hired by the telephone company, and he's voting on telephone legislation. If he got contributions from the telephone company, that wouldn't be a big story, particularly since it's a company in his district. But his wife's working there is news—partly because our whole notion of society is changing and there's a question of how independent your spouse is, and partly because it's out of the ordinary, not just a normal campaign contribution. This issue, even though it's a parochial issue, would become news if you had a similar set of circumstances.

MR. BOWER: Paul Houston listed four conflicts. Do they make a story?

MR. McCARTNEY: It's a judgment call, and my judgment would be at this point that it's not worth the time.

MR. RENNERT: You don't need personal skullduggery and cartoon-type conspiracy notions to get the story in the paper. Let me give you an example of a story that we did.

At the time of the 1968 Santa Barbara blow-out, Pauley Oil capped a few wells rather than continue to drill under the more stringent safety requirements that Interior put into effect. They lost about $70 million and tried to recoup their leases. The courts, including the Supreme Court, threw them out. Other major oil companies drilled nearby and discovered a lot of oil.

Having lost in the courts for ten years, all of a sudden Pauley Oil goes up to the Hill and a California congressman introduces legislation to give them back the lapsed leases. They hired Democratic lobbyists to lobby Democrats and Republican lobbyists to lobby Republicans. We covered the lobbyists. It was an interesting story in terms of how you influence Congress. There were lots of bucks at stake, and just the hint that there might be something not quite cricket to try to recoup after you've been through the courts. They almost got it through the Senate.

There you have hundreds of millions if not billions of dollars at stake, and you have giant pressure groups colliding. Then it's worth looking into lobbying tactics and means, and it makes a good story. But you have to raise it to that level before you get anywhere.

MR. BOWER: What we are saying, then, is that much of the work of Congress is not national news. It's basically uninteresting.

MR. HOYT: We still have that bill going through somewhere, though, and it will come to a fight. It won't be a national story, but it will interest the local media wherever that center was. That's going to be a story one way or the other. It's some of the work of Congress, and people are going to know about it.

MR. BOWER: Let's go on to the final event in the case. The day before the committee vote, the reporter finds out that the Saudis—who don't want the American oil company to develop this field—have hired Deeds's lobbying firm. But Deeds says he's never worked on the Saudi account, and he's helping Senator Smith pro bono. Is that a story?

MR. HYMEL: It makes it a story if the lobbyist resigns because he's hurting the bill, which is probably what he ought to do. A resignation gives you a news peg.

MR. FRENZEL: I don't ever see stories that take off after lobbyists because they have more than one client. Unless you can prove that somebody is slipping some grease into the game, I don't think you'd write a story like that.

MR. HOUSTON: As part of an overall story, you would include it. You don't have to suggest any wrongdoing. Deeds admits his firm works for the Saudi government but insists he doesn't work on their account; further, he insists he's working pro bono—I'd incorporate that into the story.

MR. FRENZEL: I think that's a cheap shot. It's an indictment for which there's no basis.

MR. RENNERT: You're asking the press to act on belief, and that's not our role. Our role is that when a story becomes sufficiently significant, you present the facts as best you can ascertain them and let the public judge. If I totally believed Deeds, I'd still crank it in, because I'm not the judge. The public often has the feeling that, where the reporter believes things are benign and these are really good people, he shouldn't go after them. But that presents a totally false picture of our role.

MR. FRENZEL: But the inclusion of that in your story creates the impression that somebody is playing hanky-panky here.

FRANK CHURCH AND THE SOVIET BRIGADE

MR. BOWER: Let's stay with this question of context using a different example.

On a Sunday, Frank Church [former senator, D-Idaho] was told that there were Soviet troops on maneuvers in Cuba. They had been there a long time, spread out along the island, and they were causing trouble, as soldiers will if they don't have anything else to do. In the army when that happens, you put them together and run them around until they are tired. That was the maneuvers. Senator Church had nothing else to talk about that Sunday and he gave a speech about the troops. The regional paper thought it was interesting and wrote it up. The real story was that Senator Church was in campaign trouble in Idaho. The story that got printed is that Soviet troops were on maneuvers in Cuba.

MR. McCARTNEY: No, the story was the Soviet combat brigade in Cuba. Frank was running against Steven Symms [then member of Congress, now senator, R-Idaho], and he knew he was losing. He apparently made the calculation that if he said that he was scared to death of the Soviet combat brigade in Cuba, it might move him somewhat to the right. So he made the thing public, which totally astonished the State Department and killed the Salt II treaty, which he favored, in the process. And he lost the election anyway.

MR. BOWER: But what's the story? You print anything you want regardless of your judgment as to its context or the consequences?

MR. RENNERT: I didn't say that at all. What I'm saying is, day in and day out, we write stories on imperfect knowledge. We get just a slice of the truth, not the whole truth. We are not historians twenty years later, privy to all the arguments.

MR. McPHERSON: That's disingenuous. You make decisions every day about what's relevant and not relevant. You'd write that Deeds's firm represents the Saudis, even though he doesn't himself.

MR. McCARTNEY: We were suckered. Church, as chairman of the Foreign Relations Committee, knew that it wasn't a new brigade, but he presented it to the local press in Idaho as though it was something important. He shot himself in the foot and it had immense consequences. The only way we could have put it into context, as you suggest, was to know that it wasn't new. We didn't find that out until a week later.

MR. ORNSTEIN: That's your fault. Anybody who didn't know Frank Church was running for reelection . . .

MR. McCARTNEY: We did know, and we knew he was in a lot of trouble.

MR. ORNSTEIN: And you also knew he was accessible.

MR. RENNERT: There's one trick of the trade useful in a situation like that, if he's willing to go on the record and be identified as the source instead of leaking the story. You can simply say, "Frank, are you telling me this because you're in trouble politically and you want to posture yourself as a hawkish guardian of the national security?" He would say no. Then you could put in paragraph five, "Church denied he was doing this for political purposes," and at least send a little signal to the reader to be halfway suspicious.

ADAM CLYMER [assistant to the executive editor, *New York Times*; from the audience]: You can report that there's a controversy, but just inviting somebody to deny that he beats his wife . . .

MR. RENNERT: No, no. You have instances time and again where something is very self-serving, you have a strong suspicion that the guy is not doing it pro bono, and you don't want to print just what he feeds you.

MR. CLYMER: I would want to look for somebody other than myself who will make the assertion.

MR. RENNERT: You can do that too. But at least put something in the story.

MR. HOYT: Why can't you simply report the facts under which this information was released? You don't have to make any comment about it or get him to deny he was beating his wife. Simply say he said it while in Idaho running for reelection under these circumstances.

MR. McCARTNEY: I was suckered because, although I knew the situation Church was in, I could not imagine that he would shoot down the Salt II treaty. He was one of its strongest supporters. My innocence in this case, not for the first time, got me into trouble.

MR. BOWER: So now you're pleading ignorance?

MR. McCARTNEY: I'm pleading that it was beyond my imagination that Church could have done it, because of the importance of the Salt II treaty and what the story was going to do to it.

MR. EHRENHALT: I still haven't heard how you write that story and change the situation very much. I can think of a way to write it that would make the reporter feel less guilty, but I can't think of one that would save the Salt II treaty. So you put in the paragraph in which Church said it wasn't political—exactly the same consequences. If you felt Church was being entirely mischievous, the real thing would be not to do anything with the story. That's the only way you could prevent what happened.

MR. RENNERT: No reporters that I remember had the slightest doubt about Church's accuracy. He was chairman of the Foreign Relations Committee, privy to the CIA pipeline.

HANDLING LEAKS

MR. BOWER: Let's broaden this. When you are dealing with a leak from a good source, don't you always know it is self-serving? Now, that means that the set of facts you're getting is incomplete. The story also has to do with why it's self-serving.

MR. RENNERT: The set of facts can be real and accurate. The self-serving thing is the purpose for which it is being leaked.

MR. BOWER: Which may have nothing to do with the facts. That's what happened in this situation. The purpose had to do with the election; the facts had to do with Cuba. As responsible reporters, don't you have to worry about the purpose before you print the facts?

MR. McCARTNEY: Yes.

MR. HOYT: Isn't the critical thing not the purpose, but that the facts were wrong?

MR. McCARTNEY: The facts were misrepresented.

MR. HOYT: The facts were misleading. If the facts are correct, the motive for leaking them to you is secondary.

MR. BOWER: The truth is that the facts were as presented correct but incomplete. It was true that a Soviet brigade was on maneuvers in Cuba; the reason that they were on maneuvers was not mentioned. I'm asking what you do when you get important, newsworthy leaks.

MR. McCARTNEY: You say thank you and start writing. You have to corroborate it, but you can't understand the total context of anything in life. To pretend that you can in a typical newspaper story is ridiculous.

MR. DUKE: A lot depends on what's leaked and who is doing the leaking. Say Gary Hymel tells you something in confidence about House politics. You've known him over a period of years and found him to be reliable, so you will go with it. If you get that from somebody else whose reputation you're not certain of, as a reporter you have a duty to try to pin down the facts from other sources.

MR. BOWER: Aren't you just a tool for the lobbyists or the Congressman? They will periodically give you a perfectly sound piece of information because it's in their interest to have you print it.

MR. DUKE: That may be right, but they can provide vital information so that you can write an accurate story.

MR. McCARTNEY: If you establish a rule that you can't be a tool for anybody, you'll go out of business. You're a tool all the time.

MR. HYMEL: This is the reporter's dilemma. Only sports reporters actually see what happens and report it. Everybody else has to get it filtered through somebody. You don't see what they are doing behind closed doors in the Ways and Means Committee. It's all knowing who to trust.

MR. RENNERT: If you're asking have we all lost our innocence, the answer is yes.

MR. ROBINSON: If the question is how much news does investigative journalism produce in the course of an average day for Congress, it's minimal. Congressman Frenzel told us that two of the three times he appeared on the front page were for growing and then shaving a mustache. So we are not talking about Woodward and Bernstein.

MR. RENNERT: You're putting it in an either/or context, which I reject. You seem to suggest that there's something factually suspicious about leaked information. More often than not leaked information is the most reliable information. Nevertheless, it serves somebody's purpose, and you are being used in the process.

I think the public is not aware of the extent to which it is the modus operandi at the White House. Most of the leaks in Washington are not from the Hill, but from the White House. We get background briefings where they feed us exactly the reality they want conveyed to the public. And we do it.

MR. ORNSTEIN: Let's bring it back to the case for a minute. Several things that set the context have changed in the past few years.

One is that we now have campaign finance reporting laws. There are figures at the Federal Election Commission and reporters who know how to use them. If somebody got a big campaign contribution fifteen years ago, there was no easy way for a regular Capitol Hill reporter to follow up on that. Now he can find out if the member got $300,000 in contributions from a bunch of different oil company sources. We have a huge number of campaign finance stories that never existed before.

Another change is that we now have a lot more investigative journalism. If there is a conflict of interest, bribe, or something like that, you're more likely to get a story.

A third change is the television coverage of the House. Say we move this over there, and Congressman Smith gets up on the floor and gives an emotional speech accusing the Saudi government of undermining this wonderful project. You might have a story emerge out of that because you have something visual, easy to use, and punchy. Paradoxically, you might have a story emerge in the House that would never emerge in the Senate because you don't have the visuals.

FOUR ECONOMIC STORIES

MR. BOWER: Let me push this one more step. I believe that, in general economic matters of the United States, there are about four stories. We know what they are today, and they are not going to change for a number of years. Something is news only if it affects one of those stories in a significant way. The rest is play acting, theater. We know what the nature of the deficit will be, for example. We either get at the entitlements or we don't. That's it. You can just track when something significant has been done to the entitlements. I assert that most of what you write about those issues is irrelevant. It is celebrities, conflicts, heat, fireworks, with nothing to do with underlying issues.

MR. RENNERT: I totally disagree. When you say there are only four economic stories being written—there are hundreds of economic stories being written.

MR. BOWER: About as important as this camp?

MR. RENNERT: No, much more important. I think they are being written all the time, both by national and regional press, going beyond trade, the deficit, the budget, taxes, and so on.

We have huge economic interests in this country, and I can cite stories we have written ad infinitum. People trying to get public land in northwestern California—big bucks, big companies, big lobbying. The Redwood National Forest versus the timber industry was a story that lasted for years. Umpteen stories like that don't need celebrities or the suggestion of shady dealings to get in the paper.

MR. BOWER: Just controversy?

MR. RENNERT: Collision of major interest forces.

MR. McPHERSON: Not just the fact that somebody is fighting: It really is about values. In its own way, so is the drug and oil story.

MR. BOWER: Let me stay with this. Would you accept the idea that the underlying work of Congress running the nation is boring to the extent that it doesn't represent those conflicts of value? It's the conflicts which are really interesting, because that's when values are hitting up against one another, and that's what politics is about.

MR. HOUSTON: Those are some of the most interesting stories. Some of the others simply explain what's going on with an issue or what's going on in government. The explanation function is as important as writing about conflict or collision of forces. This is particularly where the national print media excel over the electronic media.

MR. FRENZEL: I think you have carried this thing to absurdity. I could write an interesting story about the budget every day, if I could write. What is interesting to me, and what should be news, is the process. But I take it from what you're suggesting that there's only one interesting story about the budget, and if we balance it someday someone should write that story.

MR. BOWER: We are not very far apart. I'm suggesting that there is a story, and each day there's a chapter which could be written and which would be interesting and important. But that's very different from reporting a leak out of context.

MR. FRENZEL: I don't think any of us blame anybody for writing a leak. It's hard news that ought to be published if it's verifiable or reasonable. We vote on the basis of leaks all the time. And we make a hell of a lot of mistakes, just like the press does.

MR. PEARSON: What a lot of people have to understand, particularly those people who may become candidates someday, is that the work of Congress is in many instances mundane, tiresome, frustrating, and unimportant. You spend many days doing small things in little ways. These things are not reportable, and they are not of interest to anybody. What does get to be of interest is not so much a clash or conflict, but the process by which a decision is finally made. Decision making in the Congress often brings about conflicts. But by and large, things like this, even with the clash of a senator or two, or the inference of a little shady dealing, or even the involvement of big oil—which is the new devil in the land—just doesn't make it a story.

MR. EHRENHALT: One thing that struck me during this discussion is that we are interested in a lot of things. We want to know how the Ways and Means Committee works, and who is going to be Speaker five years from now. There are all kinds of stories that I like to read, and also try to write. But to assume, first, that a very large audience wants to read these stories, and, second, that in order for the republic to work well they ought to be reading these stories—that at the very least remains to be proved.

MEDIA RESOURCES

MR. BOWER: A couple of things haven't come up. All of you in the media work for a business. One question is the resources of that business. I think aside from the Associated Press and the *Washington Post*, the largest group in Washington is the *New York Times*. They have forty people that cover the federal government. How many of the forty cover the Hill?

MR. CLYMER [from the audience]: Three or four full time.

MR. BOWER: Does that have anything to do with the nature of the coverage, the issues, what gets covered and what is news?

MS. ADAMS: Of course, because you can't cover the world of the Hill with two or three people. But much of it is unimportant and uninteresting except to the people involved.

MR. BOWER: But how does your organization deal with the working of the institution over time?

MR. EHRENHALT: I work for a magazine that writes about nothing but Congress and covers things that absolutely nobody else would. That's a good question to ask people who make different kinds of decisions than we make at *Congressional Quarterly*. Everything interests us.

MR. RENNERT: My observation is that the national press and the television networks really do allocate sufficient resources. Whether they in fact use the product of those people is another question, but the *New York Times*, *Washington Post*, *Los Angeles Times*, and *Boston Globe* have good reporters and in sufficient quantity.

I'm far more concerned about the helter-skelter picture in the regional press. You have some media well represented, others not so well, and others hardly at all. There's a whole world of reporting to be done on a delegation or on individual members, both in terms of giving their constituents far more information than the national press can and in terms very often of picking up on national news. When I had John Moss [former member of Congress, D-California] investigating things left and right, I broke all kinds of national stories—the uranium cartel, gas—before the *Washington Post* and *New York Times*. It was not because I was a better reporter, but because I had John Moss. Because of Russell Long [senator, D-Louisiana], I'm sure Joan McKinney has stories on national oil policy before a lot of people in the national press.

MR. DUKE: The major newspapers are doing a better job of covering Congress than fifteen to twenty years ago. But the networks, with their enormous resources, have never allocated sufficient manpower or time to Capitol Hill. In my opinion they always overcovered the White House and undercovered Capitol Hill. As a network reporter myself, I had to fight many times to get my stories on the air and to get sufficient time to tell those stories.

In a very small way on public television we are trying to remedy this with *The Lawmakers*. We are trying to show some of the things you don't see on the networks, about how the system works and how it affects people's lives. But obviously a lot more of that is needed in television.

MS. ADAMS: Isn't there some line about people not eating sausage if they've seen how it's made? I'm not sure people should know.

MR. DUKE: They should know. But I'm not sure they want to.

6

COVERING TAX LEGISLATION
A Case Discussion

PARTICIPANTS

Christopher F. Edley, Jr. (moderator), assistant professor, Harvard Law School; former aide to President Carter

William H. Cable, partner, Williams & Jensen; former deputy assistant to President Carter for congressional Liaison

Richard E. Cohen, congressional reporter, *National Journal*

John C. Culver, former senator, D-Iowa

Richard F. Fenno, Jr., professor of political science, University of Rochester; author, *Home Style: House Members in Their Districts*

James P. Gannon, editor, *Des Moines Register*

Albert R. Hunt, Washington bureau chief, *Wall Street Journal*

Charles O. Jones, professor of government, University of Virginia; author, *The United States Congress: People, Place, and Policy*

Charles McDowell, Washington columnist, *Richmond Times-Dispatch*

Joan McKinney, Washington correspondent, *Baton Rouge Morning Advocate and State Times*

John K. Meagher, vice-president for government relations, LTD Corporation; former staff minority counsel for the House Committee on Ways and Means

Roger Mudd, Washington correspondent, NBC News

David R. Obey, member of Congress, D-Wisconsin

David Rogers, Washington bureau staff reporter, *Boston Globe*

Carole Simpson, Washington correspondent, ABC News
Pete Wilson, senator, R-California
Jonathan Wolman, Washington news editor, Associated Press

INTRODUCTORY NOTE:
This case, written by James M. Verdier, was used as the basis for the discussion.

On February 18, 1981, President Reagan announced a multi-year plan for tax cuts, domestic spending cuts, and defense spending increases. The President's tax cut proposals represented a new experiment in tax policy—marginal tax rates were to be sharply reduced in the hope that resulting increases in incentives for work, saving, and investment would stimulate enough new economic activity to offset the revenue loss that would otherwise occur. Unless this happened, or unless the Congress enacted spending cuts larger than any the Reagan administration had specifically proposed, the nation faced the prospect of high budget deficits for years to come. It was, in the words of Senate Majority Leader Howard Baker (R-Tennessee), a "riverboat gamble."

The gamble's wisdom was a matter of dispute from the beginning. The administration estimated that its plan would produce a balanced budget by fiscal year 1984, despite a proposed tax cut in that year of $118 billion. The difference would be made up by spending cuts estimated at over $100 billion and a very favorable performance by the economy. In March, however, the Congressional Budget Office (CBO) estimated that the President's proposals would lead to a $49 billion deficit in fiscal year 1984.

The controversy over economic assumptions continued throughout the spring and summer as Congress worked on its budget resolution and on administration tax and spending proposals. The Republican-controlled Senate Budget Committee used one set of assumptions, the Democratic-controlled House Budget Committee used another, and the administration used still another. Each set of assumptions produced a different set of budget estimates for future years. It was this confusion that led to administration budget director David Stockman's widely quoted remark in an Atlantic Monthly *article later in the year: "None of us really understands what's going on with all these numbers."*

The Senate Budget Committee's budget estimates ended up close to the administration's, with the committee agreeing to use similar economic assumptions and to include the administration's $44 billion in unspecified "magic asterisk" spending cuts in its projections. The House Budget Committee, however, projected a fiscal year 1984 deficit of $63 billion under the President's plan, rather than the balanced budget claimed by the administration.

The press and public paid little attention to the more pessimistic CBO and House Budget Committee estimates. Part of the reason was the fog of controversy surrounding them, with claims and counterclaims that became ever more complicated and difficult to evaluate. Another part may have been the tentativeness with which the CBO estimates were advanced. The CBO's March 25 estimate of the effects of the President's proposals cautioned that its figures were "subject to a large margin of error."

The administration bill passed and was signed into law in August. Almost immediately the experiment began to sour. The stock market dropped fifty points in August, and congressmen back in their districts found many constituents deeply distressed over high interest rates. Upon their return to Washington, congressmen had their deficit fears confirmed by a new, more confidently expressed Congressional Budget Office report, released on September 10, which projected annual deficits in the $50 billion to $60 billion range extending through 1984. The projection had a much greater public impact than the CBO's previous effort.

Specific provisions of the President's proposals also started to come under attack. A provision known as "safe-harbor leasing," which in effect allowed firms to buy and sell tax breaks, had received little coverage during debate on the bill. During August, September, and October—after the bill's enactment—major articles critical of leasing appeared in many newspapers and magazines, helping to bring about its repeal.

CHANGE IN CLIMATE

CHRISTOPHER F. EDLEY, JR.: Right after passage of the President's 1981 tax bill, many people in Congress seemed to have second thoughts. I'd like to begin by discussing why there was such a change in just a few weeks.

DAVID R. OBEY: As long as Congress was in town, everybody was busy reporting the fight and who was ahead at each furlong. There did not appear to be room on the network news for some of the questions about the economic estimates behind the program.

Then Congress got out of town, the stock market began to slide, and some of what had been printed in newspapers began to penetrate more broadly. The consequences of those numbers showed up in terms of the deficits, interest rates, and continued economic chaos. A lot of people with misgivings began to have the opportunity to move—business people who thought there was a problem but didn't want to rock the boat, because they thought it was the only boat in town; people in the Senate; even people in the administration. Those stories then began to hit the network news, which means the most in congressional districts.

When all of those doubts had been raised the first time, mighty little attention had been paid. You then had a second shot, when people started to look back at those dreary things called economic assumptions.

MR. EDLEY: Why was so little attention paid at first?

MR. OBEY: Because they were so complicated and you had a new president. The exciting question was whether this guy—who seemed to have a new style and a real idea of where he was going, in contrast to past years—was going to be able to get his way. It was reported in terms of who was going to win the ballgame.

MR. EDLEY: It was too complicated for the average journalist to get right?

MR. OBEY: Very few stories in the print media talked about those basic economic assumptions, and almost none in the electronic media. I don't know why.

MR. EDLEY: Mr. Hunt, Mr. Obey suggests that it was the complexity of the substantive story that caused the press to pay more attention to the political fight instead. Do you agree?

ALBERT R. HUNT: No, I think that was secondary. The real factor was the Democrats themselves.

The budget cuts were not the reason that the markets fell and interest rates kept going up. The budget cuts, the fairness issue, took months to appear. The problem was the size and the shape of the tax cut. Basically, the financial community realized after the fact that this was not such a hot idea.

The Democrats early on did make that case, to a very limited extent. But once the process began, what happened was not that the Democrats made their case in economic assumptions, but that Dan Rostenkowski [member of Congress, D-Illinois; chairman, Ways and Means Committee] and the Democratic leadership began a bidding war. The basic thrust of the Democratic position for those couple of months was: "We can outbid them."

We probably should have done a better job of covering the bidding war, and the fact that it and the economic assumptions were probably going to lead to great difficulties. We have our responsibilities. But politicians have their responsibilities too, and the Democrats didn't fulfill theirs.

MR. EDLEY: So one allegation is that the press didn't cover it as well as they might have, and another is that Congress, particularly the Democrats, didn't do as good a job as they might have in framing the issues for the press and the public. Why didn't the press cover the story better?

THE HONEYMOON PROBLEM

MR. HUNT: First of all, we didn't ignore the story. We agree on that. Second, there is always a problem when a new administration comes in office. The sports-writing mentality is reinforced. I plead guilty to that. But you can't ignore the fact that the people we cover are expected to make the case too. When they are not making the case, that makes it even harder for us, with all our other deficiencies.

MR. EDLEY: Mr. Obey, did you make the case?

MR. OBEY: The argument began earlier than that. Virtually every time Jim Jones [member of Congress, D-Oklahoma] and Dick Gephardt [member of Congress, D-Missouri] appeared on talk programs, anytime we had a hearing in the Budget Committee, our whole strategy was to drive home the importance of the economic assumptions. The night that the President addressed Congress, we all tried to drive home the fact that his statement about the much larger deficit under the Jones package was based on a different set of economic assumptions.

Now, I grant you that it got worse when we got into the Ways and Means Committee bidding process. I fully plead guilty, and in fact I said so in the Democratic reply. But that was only the second step. It probably increased the damage by about a third.

MR. HUNT: The whole ballgame was a tax bill.

MR. OBEY: But the budget resolution included assumptions on revenue reductions.

MR. HUNT: I know that. You were saying we had terrible problems with the economic estimates, and your leaders were saying, "If you think they're bad now, we will make them worse."

MR. OBEY: Fine, our leaders did that. But Morris Udall [member of Congress, D-Arizona], and others, and I put together a different alternative because we disagreed with the way the Democratic position was being packaged. Our package was described as the "liberal alternative"—period. That's the ink we got.

MR. EDLEY: So the press says it's Congress's responsibility to frame and explain the issues, and Congress says it's the press's responsibility to ask the right questions, to point out why the $120 billion difference is there. How can it possibly be that, on an issue of this importance, Wall Street was surprised at the shape of the tax package, and responded with a fifty-point drop? And how can it be that Congress was surprised at the reaction back on Main Street?

WAS WALL STREET SURPRISED?

JONATHAN WOLMAN: Something relatively simple was going on: the expectation on Wall Street, among the news media, and probably among the public that the President and the Democratic leadership were going to compromise. When push came to shove, the damn thing went in the other direction. It became a bidding war at the last minute. Nobody expected that every instinct to compromise on Capitol Hill would collapse in the spring of 1981.

MR. EDLEY: Mr. Cohen, do you agree with that? Were you surprised?

RICHARD E. COHEN: It became a bidding war plus a test of the President's unwillingness to compromise.

MR. EDLEY: Was the final shape of the package such a surprise that the press can be excused for not having adequately communicated, to Wall Street and to Main Street, what was about to come down and what its implications were?

MR. COHEN: To some extent it was a surprise. But was it the press's responsibility to tell the public that a three-year bill at 25 percent would be a greater problem than a two-year bill at X percent?

MR. EDLEY: You're implying that you don't think it was the press's responsibility.

MR. COHEN: We just report what other people are doing.

MR. EDLEY: But the proposal was there.

MR. COHEN: And there were various actors in Congress who dealt with that bill. It was their responsibility to state their views on it. Some Democrats said there were serious problems, and there was some coverage of that. I'm sure Dave Obey is correct, there should have been more. But part of the problem was that not enough of the Democrats had their act together in presenting the message. It was Dan Rostenkowski saying one thing, Obey and Henry Reuss [member of Congress, D-Wisconsin] and Udall saying another, and the boll-weevils saying something else.

It was hard to figure out whether what the Obey crowd was saying deserved the most attention. Now, obviously, he looks good, and I think he was right. But it may not have been clear then, because the message from the Democrats was so diffused.

MR. EDLEY: A big, messy, complicated, diffused issue—whose responsibility is it to clarify it for the public?

MR. COHEN: You can't clarify mud.

DAVID ROGERS: You have to deal with some of the context here. This business of Reagan's deficit didn't begin with Jim Jones, it began with George Bush's calling it "voodoo economics." That hadn't changed. Also, the Democrats lost badly in 1980. They came in scared. They had a very narrow margin in the House, and the vote was soft.

One of the problems with Jim Jones's economic statistics was that he was too optimistic, too. It wasn't that Jim Jones had the truth and the Republicans didn't; Jim Jones had a more pessimistic forecast which in the end proved to be more accurate. But it was not as if he really staked out a clear position.

You have to deal with Wall Street, too. They were up to their neck in it. Anyone who thinks that Wall Street didn't know is crazy, and it isn't because of the press. They knew all along. They had their own interests in certain tax benefits, and once they got them, then they complained about the deficits. Also, it's a function of more than the tax policy. It's also a function of the military policy that Wall Street may not have been as comfortable with. And, in fairness to Jack Kemp—not that I would want to overdo it—the monetary policy of that summer has to be considered as well.

So it was several things coming together. It isn't as if the tax bill brought the recession. The argument can be made that the monetary policy plus the tax bill plus the military policy may have brought it.

MR. EDLEY: Given the kind of coverage that existed, should a reasonably diligent reader have been surprised by the deficit estimates that started coming out in August and September?

MR. ROGERS: No.

MR. EDLEY: Anybody disagree with that?

JOAN McKINNEY: I think the differences in economic assumptions were reported, accurately and repeatedly. But the media did not say that one set of economic assumptions was right. They didn't do that for the same reason that economists can't do that.

So I don't think the public was particularly surprised. The public was probably pretty divided going in, and they figured we were going to find out pretty soon which assumptions were right.

RIVERBOAT GAMBLE

MR. EDLEY: Did the media do a good enough job of alerting the public to the dimensions of what Howard Baker called the "riverboat gamble?" Did people really appreciate how divided the opinion was among the experts?

MR. HUNT: Now that we know what has happened, I don't think anyone in our business would say we did an effective enough job. But don't get caught in this black-and-white situation where if only the press had said the deficit would be $172.3 billion next year, then everything would have been fine. It wouldn't have been.

Howard Baker did say it's going to be a riverboat gamble, and he went on to say it's going to work, there will be more people back at work, the country will have a new sense of spirit, it will be the greatest thing since sliced bread. The notion that during all this time there were a whole bunch of warnings being raised is exaggerated, David Obey and Mo Udall notwithstanding.

MR. OBEY: We thought we had the votes for the Jones budget, which contained revenue reductions, when we left town for the recess. What we did was give the White House a crucial week to turn it around through their business calls. We also faced Reagan's speech, when he hammered on virtually one item, the deficit. And Jones, in his attempt to respond to that, was absolutely wiped out. We were all wiped out on that point: You couldn't tell whose deficit was going to be larger because he was using one set of economic assumptions to describe his and another one to describe ours. It's a tough point for anybody to get across, press or politician. We certainly didn't get it across, and we didn't get a hell of a lot of help—not in persuading people our estimates were right, but just in explaining that the estimates determined what was going to happen.

MR. EDLEY: Ms. Simpson, did you do a story on the differences in economic assumptions?

CAROLE SIMPSON: No.

MR. EDLEY: Why not?

MS. SIMPSON: I was covering the House for NBC, and tax legislation is what we call a MEGO story: "My Eyes Glaze Over." For television it is almost impossible to make any sense of tax legislation and help the public understand it.

MR. EDLEY: Is it inevitably a MEGO story that you shouldn't touch with a ten-foot pole?

MS. SIMPSON: I'm not saying we didn't touch it. I covered it, but again it was in the sense of the horse-race. This was Reagan's first year in office. He came in saying he was going to cut taxes and balance the budget and cut federal spending, and those were the major things we were looking at. Is he going to accomplish these things?

MR. EDLEY: But on the basic issue of whether the President's proposal is going to drive up the deficits and wreck the economy?

MS. SIMPSON: We put on Democrats expressing the point of view that this would be dangerous, that it would create huge deficits. And we had Republicans saying that this is the way to go, that it will stimulate the economy.

MR. EDLEY: Is there anything that can be faulted in the television coverage?

UNINTERESTED AUDIENCES

MS. SIMPSON: Yes. We have talked about the failings of Congress and the failings of reporters. But we have not talked about the failings of the American public.

Let me tell you about some of the letters I've gotten. "You ought to smile more." No one knows what I've said about the tax bill, but they like to see me wearing red. And this is a network news audience, generally considered more sophisticated than the audience watching prime-time television and sitcoms and local news. This is supposed to be the better-educated, the more well-off.

They are not interested. Every time you try to put on a three-hour documentary about energy, what kind of ratings does it get? If you look at the market research on what people like to see on television news, it's the features, the things involving celebrities. Our producers and our editors are responsive to that.

JAMES P. GANNON: You've defined the problem for television: market surveys. I just reject the notion.

MR. EDLEY: Newspapers don't have this problem?

MR. GANNON: I do market surveys on what people are interested in. But mine are apparently a lot different than yours, because they show that people are interested in national and international news.

MR. SIMPSON: You have a more literate audience. You have readers.

MR. COHEN: I think there's an assumption here: If we had more readers who knew what was going on, if we were able to figure out that the Obey assumptions were correct, and if we had really came on strong and said the Reagan stuff is mush, then that would have made for a different result in the House. I'm not sure that's correct.

MR. OBEY: The problem with the press was that you expected us to do both things at the same time. We had the narrowest partisan margin in modern history in that House. We were being kicked because the Jones alternative was not sufficiently different from the Reagan one, yet at the same time we were being kicked because we weren't winning. The Democrats couldn't beat the administration budget and still be greatly different.

MR. ROGERS: You're defining your goal in terms of winning.

MR. OBEY: I'm saying that Jones had to fight on the edges.

MR. ROGERS: Jones did not have a substantially greater claim to truth than Reagan at the time. Jones was closer for sure, and to the extent he was closer he had more. But Jones was cutting the margins. He was trying to hold onto some boll-weevils in committee.

Don't go back and look at this as a great economic debate. The fact is, the people we were covering were interested in preserving some margins.

MR. EDLEY: Is your argument that because everything was margins, it wasn't newsworthy?

MR. ROGERS: I considered that to be terrifically newsworthy. I don't think anyone had any trouble interesting readers in a three-year tax bill. But to go back and say the press didn't look at the debate in terms of economics ignores the fact that all the players were looking at it in terms of maintaining certain margins and winning. I think the press looked at maintaining the margins too.

ROLE-PLAYING

MR. HUNT: Congressman Obey, you act as if we only had a four- or five-month debate over this tax plan. There were Republicans talking about it for three or four years. Ronald Reagan never hid the fact that he was going to have a huge tax cut. Nobody should have been surprised. You can sit here in 1983 and say it didn't work—and I may think you're right—but in 1981 Ronald Reagan did exactly what he said he was going to do.

MR. OBEY: The question I was asked at the beginning was why it caused the change in climate that allowed Congress to go back and redo a portion of what it did. When we were first dealing with it, Reagan was the shining knight. It was exciting to see whether he was going to be able to turn the whole dog-gone political system around. The press focused on that and we got bagged, in my judgment. We were expected to perform the function of a parliamentary majority, to pass something different, at the same time that we were expected to point out that the facts it was based on were terrible. We couldn't do both at the same time, so we were politically disadvantaged.

That's not your fault. If we hadn't been elected to a majority we would have had a much greater ability to state the differences. But we had to play a two-track game; we had in effect to role play. Jones had to try to win. I took the other role, which was to lay out the major problems with the package.

RICHARD F. FENNO, JR.: The media shouldn't be defensive about the horse race. There are times when that is the story, and it seems to me that it was the story in that early period. The question has to do with the length of the honeymoon.

MR. EDLEY: Are you arguing that the horse race was as important as the question of whether or not there was going to be a $250-billion deficit?

MR. FENNO: I think the public was interested in giving the President a chance.

MR. EDLEY: Does everybody agree with that?

MS. McKINNEY: When the President asked people to call their congressmen, he asked it in terms of: "This is what I told you I wanted to do in the campaign, and I'm in danger of Congress not letting me do it." He asked them to call their congressional offices, and they did it by the hundreds. They were talking in very simplistic terms: "Give the man a chance."

DIFFERENT STANDARDS FOR TELEVISION

ROGER MUDD: The whole thing for me is really a dusty swirl. I don't remember nine-tenths of what these people say happened. The reason I don't remember is that none of it was on television. And, probably, none of it will ever get on television because, aside from whatever the audience's appetite is for knowing what its taxes will be, television is simply incapable of handling this kind of discussion and this kind of issue.

Just in fairness to television, I propose that it not be judged by the same standards as the press. It's an altogether different instrument. It strikes at different emotions, at a different part of the brain. It's powerful at certain times and hopelessly weak at others. This is not a story that ever is going to get on television.

JOHN C. CULVER: In the election, the American public wanted to believe that Reagan had a formulation that would bring about this economic recovery. Once he received their endorsement, the public felt he ought to have the opportunity to put it across. I think that was the story. Jones's numbers, Obey's numbers, anybody's numbers notwithstanding, that was the essence of the story.

MR. EDLEY: Let me state this as pointedly as I can. The issue for me is, do you defer to what your audience is interested in, or do you try to lead opinion? So what if they are interested in the horse race—what does the horse-race have to do with whether people are going to end up unemployed, or what the interest rates are going to be?

MR. COHEN: Ultimately we have to rely on and report on what the politicians we cover are talking about. The most interesting part of the 1981 tax debate and what happened after July was that it wasn't the Democrats who opened the issue up again for broad discussion; it was the Republicans in the Senate. They swallowed their doubts until the tax bill was passed. Immediately when they came back, Pete Domenici [senator, R-New Mexico] wanted to undo what he had been forced to do because the Reagan White House wouldn't give. That shows their great doubts. Domenici was very clear on that.

MR. HUNT: If it doesn't matter who wins or loses, then why keep score? It did matter. It mattered, not just because of policy, but because of the whole sense of governance. Could a new President come in and do things? Did the fact that forty-four out of fifty states voted for this fellow matter? Could Republicans be the governing party? All of those are very important questions, just as important in their own respect as the size of the budget deficit. I think we make a huge mistake if we try to say it's an either-or position.

MR. MUDD: We say the Supreme Court follows the flag; I think the press follows the flag too. It was reporting, in the context of the President's promises and performance, a story that would be a good measure of whether he was going to live up to what he said.

MR. HUNT: Having just followed an administration widely thought to be impotent.

A RADICAL CHANGE

CHARLES McDOWELL: In a news column that runs in a remote place, I tried to take on this issue. With the so-called Reagan mandate—which I think wasn't quite the mandate we thought it was—I saw this being fought by the Democrats in terms of numbers, and I saw the press doing its job reporting it. I knew that there was a point to make, and I don't think it ever got made by the Democrats and the press.

Keeping the numbers out of it, this was a very radical thing that Reagan brought in. And we covered the horse race. What we never did, it seems to me—and I tried—was to say: This budget ain't balanced. It's hugely not balanced. I quoted Jack Kemp once a week: "We no longer worship at the shrine of a balanced budget." I dealt in big, dumb terms.

MR. EDLEY: To convey the sense that this was radical?

MR. McDOWELL: To convey the notion that this is a big deal, and their little budget differences are going to get dismissed as trivial. The people were never told we were undergoing historic change in how the Republican Party approaches budgets. "We no longer worship at the shrine of a balanced budget" is a remarkable announcement.

We got caught up in covering the horse race. The President wanted to do well and people wanted him to do well—we covered that. But we never got across to people: This is an historic turnaround, folks, and if you're going to buy it, you're going to buy voodoo economics.

MR. EDLEY: Senator Wilson, Mr. McDowell comes to you and sticks his cassette recorder up in your face and says, "Do you understand how radical this is?" What do you say?

PETE WILSON: I say, "Charlie, you're absolutely right. It is a departure."

There are two legitimate stories here. The horse race is legitimate; it should have been covered, and it was. The far more difficult story is the other one. When you ask if the American people are interested in a tax cut story, you bet they are. They may not be as interested in detail of economic assumptions; there is a lot of MEGO. But when you ask if the press had an obligation to tell their readers what they should be interested in—that's a noble undertaking that I don't see occurring. I see people comparing ratings.

MR. EDLEY: And that's okay so far as you're concerned?

MR. WILSON: No, it isn't okay. Unhappily, it's a fact of life. There's too much emphasis on the horse race.

But you have different kinds of media. A large newspaper can be both *MacNeil-Lehrer* and the network news. It can offer its readers what they want. Some will read one, and some will read both, and some will read neither and skip to the sports page. But if you're talking about economic assumptions, then you're talking about the necessity for a *MacNeil-Lehrer* approach.

MR. EDLEY: Suppose Mr. McDowell, with the microphone in

your face, says, "Why is it you tend to believe this set of economic assumptions rather than that set?"

MR. WILSON: If it were Charlie, I would ask how many inches we have. If it were Roger and I know we have thirty or forty-five seconds, I'd be hard-pressed. I would have to have thought about it beforehand. Not just thought about it, but thought about it in a way that would allow me to use big, plain terms.

FOLLOWING THE LEADER

MR. EDLEY: Turn to a somewhat different issue, accountability. Mr. McDowell, suppose you approach some senator and ask that question. He shrugs and says, "Well, I have colleagues whom I respect, and they are experts on this. I can't be an expert on everything, so I go along with them." Is that a news story?

MR. McDOWELL: It is if he will answer the next question: "Is it not true, then, sir, that the Republican Party has completely turned over its whole assumption about budgets, and that you have turned over your whole life history in politics as a balanced-budget man?" If he will deal with that, then that's what I can write.

MR. MUDD: If the Senator says he doesn't really know the answer but he's going along with Culver, I think that's a story. What is the guy doing in the Senate?

MR. COHEN: I think we ran the story in 1981 that the Republican Senate marched in lock-step formation for Reagan. They had their internal doubts, but they did it. That was a big story, and we made it pretty clear.

MR. CULVER: That wasn't the issue as I recall it. The issue was really that the President and these Kemp-Roth advocates weren't conceding there's going to be red ink indefinitely. They said: "Ye of little faith, be prepared for some short-term deficits, but the magic of this formulation is going to trigger all these other wondrous things, and, behold, the Treasury will have a tough time accommodating all the additional money that's going to be pouring in, and therefore we are going to balance it in two or three quick years."

It was a question of whether you were a true believer. That was the issue, and it came down to the politics of it. These members had seen everybody go down in 1980 over the same debate.

MR. EDLEY: Did you go to anybody in your delegation and say, "Look, how much do you know about what's going on in this? How much do you appreciate the gamble, the risks, the stakes involved?"

MS. McKINNEY: I don't think I put it in exactly those terms. I was dealing with members who claimed to know the stakes involved, basically because most of them had been part of the boll-weevil caucus that claimed to be doing exhaustive studies on all of this. It would be rather silly of me to tell Russell Long [Senator, D-Louisiana] he didn't know what was involved.

JOHN K. MEAGHER: You're suggesting that the press has some moral obligation to lobby members of Congress by printing certain stories. I don't think that's the case at all. The issue here is that in certain instances we all use the press. The leasing question is a perfect example, where Dole used the press to kill safe-harbor leasing and those of us on the other side were behind that public-relations curve. But to suggest that the reporter should go to the delegation and browbeat the members into taking what the reporter considers a responsible position—I just think that's crazy.

MR. McDOWELL: Our obligation was to say, "As you take this riverboat gamble, do you acknowledge that it is a riverboat gamble?" That's a fair question, not to lobby them but to get them to admit what they were doing, and I think it was too seldom asked.

MR. HUNT: In 1979 and 1980, Ronald Reagan and most Republicans said: "We will do three things for you. Number one, we are going to have the most massive defense build-up this country has ever seen. Number two, we are going to have a tax cut like you wouldn't dream. Number three, we are going to balance the budget." And it was going to work because someone has a napkin with a curve.

I don't think they hid that message. My editorial writers went crazy and said, "Isn't that hosanna, it's going to be wonderful." The press wrote about it. The John Culvers and Jimmy Carters and Dave Obeys made the opposite case, and for whatever reason people didn't buy it.

SAFE-HARBOR LEASING

MR. EDLEY: Let's shift gears a little bit. The bill is passed; it's the fall of 1981. A group called Citizens for Tax Justice Now writes a press blurb about safe-harbor leasing, with six or seven examples of large corporations gaining lots of tax benefits as a result of the provisions. They write a letter to Chairman Rostenkowski and demand a hearing. Mr. Meagher, let's assume for the moment that you represent a company that takes advantage of these safe-harbor leasing provisions. Do you want there to be a hearing?

MR. MEAGHER: No.

MR. EDLEY: Why not?

MR. MEAGHER: Because I have what I want, and I want to keep it.

MR. EDLEY: A hearing is a risk to you?

MR. MEAGHER: Of course.

MR. EDLEY: Suppose your client says, "Try to get to Rostenkowski and, if you can't get him to cancel the hearing, at least try to get him to shape the hearing in a way that's responsible." So you call Rostenkowski's office. Are you going to be able to get in to see him?

MR. MEAGHER: Sure. But that's not what happened.

MR. EDLEY: Wait. He's going to have a hearing. You're trying to influence it somehow. What do you want him to do?

MR. MEAGHER: Obviously what I want is a hearing that isn't stacked from either side, unless it's mine. What I really want is to make sure that the merits of the proposal are debated fairly, and that the side that's attacking it doesn't have fifteen witnesses to the three who are defending it.

MR. EDLEY: You'll feed him the names of possible witnesses, to help present a balanced case?

MR. MEAGHER: Yes.

WINNING BY LOSING

MR. ROGERS: John Meagher played a major role in the leasing debate, educating members of the press too.

MR. EDLEY: You worked the press?

MR. MEAGHER: Yes. I can tell you about the strategy, to take it out of the hypothetical. One news story created an image that this was corporate welfare, and it was picked up all over the country. It was an impossible job to get to the merits of the issue after that occurred. But I spent most of my time on this thing talking to the press, trying to educate them as to its merits.

MR. EDLEY: Why was it so difficult to persuade reporters of the merits of your side?

MR. MEAGHER: Maybe the real reason is that we were wrong, but I don't think so. An even more fundamental question, very complicated and difficult to deal with, is what you do about the problem that occasioned safe-harbor leasing. There is a very difficult tax problem; I don't think many people in the tax world would disagree with that. The disagreement has been over the solution. And the solution of safe-harbor leasing simply didn't play well in Peoria.

But the result was that those that really made out under it—the companies that bought the tax credits—ended up being the ones that ultimately won. They were criticized for having taken advantage of the law, and when safe-harbor leasing was repealed they ended up in a much better position than before.

MR. EDLEY: The story that appeared about the companies that were making a bundle off safe-harbor leasing, and how successful they had been in getting the provision in—was that a good story?

MR. GANNON: Sure. There was only one thing wrong with it: It was six months too late.

MR. EDLEY: Why didn't it come six months earlier?

MR. GANNON: That's the key question here. Why did we learn about the implications of safe-harbor leasing after the bill was passed? Why didn't we learn about it while you guys were doing what you were doing?

TOO MUCH AT ONCE

MR. MEAGHER: The answer is that the issue in the tax bill was not safe-harbor leasing. There were several issues when the tax bill went through: the thirty percent across-the-board tax cut, indexing, royalty payments. It was lost in the shuffle. This was proposed by the administration, by the way; it wasn't something that just came out of the blue. It got in as part of a tremendous package. Those of us in favor of it certainly didn't go around telling the press. Do I want coverage when I've got something? No. I want to go play golf.

MR. EDLEY: Do you accept that defense offered on your behalf?

MR. GANNON: I understand the explanation but I don't consider it a justification. It doesn't get the press off the hook as far as I'm concerned. When the sophisticated press—the *Wall Street Journal*, *New York Times*, and *Los Angeles Times*—can't find that story, or ignores that story until the bill is passed, then I think the press failed.

MR. HUNT: A couple of points have to be kept in mind. First, there was a whole bunch of stuff going on. We are talking about a multi-billion-dollar tax bill, and this was just part of it. Second, the reason it became a big issue was because by the fall the whole fairness issue began to come out. Before the fairness issue, there were tax breaks for rich people all the time—MEGO stories. But once the fairness issue came out, a bunch of corporations swapping tax breaks became a much bigger story. You have to keep it in context—which is not to excuse us, but it really does make it different.

MR. McDOWELL: Was anybody onto this? Or did nobody in the whole nation report it?

MR. HUNT: We wrote about it as the story evolved. We just didn't make a big deal about a bunch of rich corporations swapping tax breaks. As the bill was passing, we were writing about it.

MR. EDLEY: Mr. Cable, do you think the people who were writing those stories really understood the substantive issues involved?

WILLIAM H. CABLE: I think the *Wall Street Journal* story [August 27, 1981] described the substantive issue very well. It's a very good, factual story.

USING THE PRESS TO LOBBY

MR. McDOWELL: Would that story have affected anything if it had come out earlier?

MR. MEAGHER: I don't think so. I really believe it was caught up in a large tax bill. It was a blip on the screen.

There's another thing that this group ought to address: the extent to which the press is used. Most people today in the lobbying business have media strategies as well as Hill strategies. The most important paper for a lobbyist is the *Washington Post*, simply because everybody on Capitol Hill can read it that day. You cannot, by any other means short of spending millions of dollars, get the same kind of influence—unless Roger Mudd carries it, and not everybody will see that. But it can cut both ways, as it did in safe-harbor leasing. Get a bad story and you're playing catch-up ball from then on.

What is the role of the press's being used, either by interests or by members of Congress who want to get a particular point of view across or a particular bill passed?

MS. SIMPSON: We are used by everybody. We are used by consumer groups, by the people who demonstrate on the mall. That's our role.

MS. McKINNEY: Let me suggest a human element here that may have come into play with safe-harbor leasing. You feel bad enough when you miss a story. If you feel that you missed it because you've been abused, you've been deliberately misled, you may tend to overreact to recover lost ground. We are intensely conscious of being used, and there are times when it can backfire.

MR. EDLEY: This is about the seventh time today that somebody on the press side has talked about the problem of being used, the problem of being seduced by staged events.

MS. McKINNEY: I don't resent it when I'm receiving something from a lobbyist or a member of Congress, even if they initiated it. I understand they have a viewpoint and a reason for presenting it to me, and I then have an obligation to look at the accuracy of the material and their motive, and to search for whether there is a different viewpoint. I just consider it part of the information-gathering process.

I think television people are more worried about it than print people, perhaps because just the presence of the camera and the television crew changes the nature of the event—in fact the event may be happening because of television. Conscientious television people are very worried about that. The one elementary thing you do in writing a story is not to rely on only one source of information. It's different for television people who have constraints that we don't have.

MS. SIMPSON: Television needs pictures and everybody knows it. The Republicans on the Hill are quite successful, like the giant apple pie at the Washington Monument that every television camera in town went out to shoot. And we all took helicopters and shot the giant American flag that was spread out there. I was covering the nutrition committee, and they had found out Americans consumed 350 cans of soda pop a year. They realized that might not get coverage, so they brought in 350 cans of soda pop. It made a very dramatic picture, and television covered it. Because we are looking for ways to make our stories interesting and visual, we are often used that way.

MR. EDLEY: I guess the bottom-line question is, are your needs immutable? Or are they simply the way you've grown up in the business, part of the lore of the profession?

MR. MUDD: What Carole says is true most of the time for television, but occasionally we can get along without pictures. We got along without them in Watergate. Night after night we covered Watergate with talking heads because there was nothing to film, no pictures of garages or of the *New York Times* stuffed in the flower pot, just Daniel Schorr and Lesley Stahl talking. If the issue is major, if it goes to the very heart of the democratic process, we can report it without pictures. *MacNeil-Lehrer* has done it for a long time, and they do it pretty well.

MS. SIMPSON: Don't you think, with the state of the art of computer graphics, an attempt would be made now to illustrate the Watergate story?

MR. MUDD: Graphics don't really help. All they do is make the screen move around a lot.

MR. JONES: It seems to me that the case adds up to this: there is a question about the effectiveness of the press when political dynamics are moving faster than even the members can control. The press tends to contribute to the momentum. It fails to set down warning signals, or even to see how revolutionary the action may be.

But I remember that on some television programs there was discussion of the revolutionary impact of the tax cut, the commitments that were involved, the deficit-paying that was going to be done later on. The media's warning signals may be inconsequential because of the momentum.

UNFINISHED BUSINESS

MR. EDLEY: Let me wrap this up by listing several things we haven't gotten closure on.

There are needs of broadcast journalism and of print journalism, but the needs are flexible. There's some give, depending on how important the story is. We didn't explore how flexible the needs are, and whether they are wholly internal to journalists' narrow, perhaps parochial, views about their role. That's number one.

Number two is the question of the judgments that the media make about what the audience wants to hear as opposed to what the audience ought to hear, and whether the press ought to be more aggressive in making non-market-related decisions about what it reports.

A third issue that we thought about a bit is the question of responsibility for clarifying and explaining information, the relative responsibilities of people in Congress and the people who are covering it. If even the diligent public remains confused about economic assumptions, about the magnitude of the riverboat gamble, about the substantive merits of leasing, is that the fault of Congress? To what extent is it the responsibility of the media to try to make something clear despite its murkiness? We had a lot of finger-pointing, but we didn't have any agreement as to the bottom line on responsibility. Maybe there's no such thing.

MR. ROGERS: This is not really a question of Congress, the media, and the political relationship between the two, nor is it a morality play where the issue is who told whom. The fact is, your function is to report. The fact is, the story was a major political shift, born out of the 1980 election, which went one way in a very large way and then adjusted itself somewhat. But it didn't go all the way back and change the second or third year of the tax cut, and this year once again they didn't change that.

The debate was not about the truth of economic assumptions. It was about the political balance that was reflected in margins in which the Jones budget was different than Gramm-Latta. In fact the Jones budget was not as important as the budget reconciliation bill or the tax debate. All that was margin. I think in your desire to get generalizations, you're not dealing with that political story and how we intermeshed with it.

MR. EDLEY: That's interesting because I would have thought that, if we had learned anything by the discussion today, it's that any assertion that begins with "The story is" must be incredibly subjective. You make the story; life doesn't make the story.

7

NEWS JUDGMENT AND CONGRESS
A Speech by Senator Bob Dole

The media, I believe, have a growing responsibility as they relate to Congress. You are our most important, direct link to the American people, and we are very concerned about that. Sometimes we think the news is biased. Sometimes you think we are biased. Many things done by members of Congress—I'll not exclude this member—tend to be self-serving, but this isn't the norm as I see it. Some may think that most members of the press are liberal and Democratic, and they may be right. Nonetheless, we generally find very objective reporting when those of us with some responsibility make ourselves accessible.

When I first came to Congress about twenty-three years ago, we never thought of calling a press conference. It wouldn't have done any good, come to think of it—nobody would have come. There wasn't a member of Congress, on either side, who would ever say anything that might upset the ranking member. I didn't dare put out a release before checking with somebody who was superior to me. And for a long time that was everybody on our side.

Since 1961, there has been a massive change, and it's a change for the better. But I think we are going to have to figure out some way, not to control the press or to control the Congress, but to have better interaction so that you can sort out the news.

THE MAJORITY DIFFERENCE

I recall being in the minority, as a Republican in the Senate, and wondering why the party never had adequate coverage. The primary reason was that we weren't available. We didn't want to talk about anything. We said it once and thought it ought to be etched in stone. We never really learned you have to repeat and repeat.

There's a vast difference between being in the minority and being in the majority. You can be very comfortable in the minority by just voting against everything, putting out a release saying how bad it is, and letting somebody else have the responsibility for its passage. If it works nobody cares, and if it fails you can say, "I told you it wouldn't work." Conversely, in the majority you find yourself in a position of either trying to make something happen or joining the nay-sayers and just letting it stagnate.

Sometimes I don't envy my House Republican colleagues, who seem to find it easy to say, "We don't want to do this." They have a great deal of influence, and sometimes it's frustrating. But it's a different perspective. In the minority, nobody wants to talk to you unless you're the ranking member of the party. But if you're in the majority and a committee chairman, you have a strong responsibility to be accessible and to try to make certain that what you do is, for the most part, objective and balanced.

THE ACCESS DILEMMA

I don't understand the definition of news. But I suggest there may be a lot of minor stories passing for headline news these days, and a lot of potential news that doesn't make it at all.

I was a member of the Gang of Seventeen, trying to put together a budget package. We decided we would have secret meetings, which we knew would probably interest the press. We didn't have anything to talk about, but we thought we ought to keep it secret in case something came up. So we had fifteen or sixteen meetings to discuss the economy, and it generally took us thirty minutes to tell how we ducked the press. I remember being chased out of the garage. When I was a candidate for president, I didn't have anybody chasing me, especially not the press. We were always followed by cars, tracked by motorcycles, and pursued by undercover agents. Jim Jones [member of Congress, D-Oklahoma; chairman, Budget Committee] was interviewed while he pedaled his bicycle to Blair House. He has been riding it ever since, because he made the nightly news, but nobody has stopped him.

There was the question of access, of whether to let the press know what's happening or to back off and wait until we had a product. We made a pledge to ourselves in the first meeting that if we had any budget resolution, whether Democratic or Republican, we would keep our mouths shut. That's very hard for somebody in politics, but we did it. So about all the press could speculate on was whether the meeting was going to break down, not what we were discussing. They would predict the meeting was breaking down if the members came out and didn't look too happy.

I'm not certain we ever told the American people how important those sessions were. That's the problem of access. If you give access and the features of your plan get out, somebody is going to shoot it down. If you don't give access, nobody is going to know what it is and they will think Congress is trying to sneak something through.

PRIME-TIME AMENDMENTS

Public opinion, I think, is often already shaped by the media before we get a chance to deal with it. Somebody takes a poll, or twenty minutes out of the nightly news is about Grenada or Lebanon, and opinions are formed almost so quickly that Congress has no real chance to respond. We start organizing and planning and scheming, not to lead public opinion, but to get on the right side so we can follow public opinion.

For example, a lot of my colleagues were very concerned that we were doing the wrong thing in Grenada. A lot of people in Congress were planning to attack somebody, but before they did the students came back, kissed the ground, and applauded the President and everyone else. It turned out to be a fairly popular move after all. Without the media there to tell us how the students wanted to come home, it was pretty difficult to do the right thing—whatever the right thing was. There are some members still groping for that.

That's why we had to get back to the debt ceiling. I'd like to get off it. On Thursday we brought it up, and we thought we would dispose of it very quickly. We have been on it Thursday and Friday and Saturday. We don't meet tomorrow but we have a meeting to try to put together the budget resolution.

We have had a number of amendments to the debt ceiling, which have no relevance to it. We had one this morning on some secret fund for Jordan, which I accepted without a vote because I didn't understand it and I couldn't find anybody who did. It has nothing to do with my jurisdiction. Yesterday, Howard Baker [senator, R-Tennessee] offered an amendment praising the President, and then Robert Byrd [senator, D-West Virginia] offered one condemning the President. They finally decided to pull them both. That was very helpful to the budget process. The War Powers Act was added on to the debt ceiling yesterday. I voted for it; it seemed to me it might be a good thing to do. We are going to have one on abortion and one on the nuclear freeze, too. It becomes sort of a turkey shoot. Anybody with an amendment he doesn't know what to do with offers it on the debt ceiling.

There are going to be a lot of headlines written about all these amendments, but they aren't going anywhere. The amendments will be lucky to make it to the conference committee, because they are not germane. When I sit down with my counterpart, Dan Rostenkowski [member of Congress, D-Illinois; chairman, Ways and Means Committee], the first thing we will do is dump the amendments that don't deal with the debt ceiling. But there will be a lot of nice television coverage and stories written first.

These are what we call "prime-time amendments." They are the ones you offer between 2:30 and 4:30 p.m. on a normal day, which is about right for the evening news. Sometimes you have people competing for the prime-time amendments. You can't choose among your friends, so you let them each offer a prime-time amendment or a prime-time substitute. Then everybody has a fair shot at the evening news. We try not to disappoint people.

You've got to figure out which is real and which is not. It's very difficult. But I don't think we fool you.

UNTOLD STORIES: SOCIAL SECURITY AND THE DEFICIT

But I'm not so certain you fool us either. We are searching for ways to be better members of Congress, but the media doesn't wait for anyone. It's all so quick that members sometimes wonder if you are really covering the news. I want to give a couple of examples.

Let's take the Social Security bill of last year. I won't spend a lot of time on detail. You're in the news business; detail is not your bag.

In 1981 there was a broad feeling among Democrats and Republicans that we ought to do something about Social Security. Then the White House made a mistake and unveiled their plan prematurely, because Claude Pepper [member of Congress, D-Florida; Chairman, Select Committee on Aging] wanted to see what they were doing. Some of the things looked like they might be going after senior citizens, and that caused an uproar in April of 1981. Before long it had gone from restraint on the growth of COLAs [cost of living adjustments] to cutting benefits.

The White House panicked and appointed a commission. In my view we already had a commission, Congress, but they didn't want to face up to Social Security, so the White House appointed a new commission. I was on it. We had a big media event the first time we met, and then a lot of dry discussion at seven or eight other meetings when the media didn't show up.

To the credit of a lot of reporters, they did some objective stories on the Social Security problem—what it was, how bad it was, what Congress might do about it. But the result, from a political standpoint, was that twenty-six Republicans lost seats in 1982, and about three or four Senate candidates didn't win who should have won. I don't suggest they all lost because of Social Security. But exit polling indicated that a number of them lost because voters felt Republicans were going to cut benefits. That's what Claude Pepper told them, and they believed Claude Pepper. I don't know how we address that. I don't believe the Social Security story was ever told.

Now we are into another one, budget deficits. It's very difficult, with all the foreign policy questions, for the media to have time to focus on anything else. In fact, I had a press conference the other day to talk about a $120-billion deficit reduction package, and the networks couldn't come. That was all right with us. Nobody wanted their name on the deficit reduction measure. I wasn't sure I did, but we had to have somebody's name on it.

I can't think of a more serious problem right now than budget deficits. We can blame the President or we can blame past Democratic administrations all we want. But the point is, if we don't do something the national debt will double in the next four or five or six years, from $1.3 trillion to $2.5 trillion, with $250 billion annual interest. That doesn't create a single job, doesn't help a single university, farmer, student, or anybody in this country. The interest payment is more than the whole debt was in 1972.

That's the biggest domestic story in this country. It's something you can't take pictures of, something that's very difficult for people to comprehend in a thirty-second or a fifty-second bite, whatever those things are. But I can't think of a more important story that hasn't been told. We are not asking for support. We are asking somebody to take a look at this problem in an objective way. Separate it from the politics. Maybe that's not the media's responsibility. But it is an untold story in many ways.

THE CAMERA'S IMPACT

Congress is a different kind of world altogether now. They have television in the House, and Senator Baker wants television in the Senate. Our theory is that he's leaving, he won't need it, so there's no rush. I don't think it will happen in the Senate for a while, because some people don't want it. Democrats don't want it as long as Republicans are in charge, and we won't want it when they are in charge.

That's part of the problem, the political problem. I would like to go into closed session next week and have a mark-up. I could mark up our bill on revenue, on deficit reduction, in half the time in closed session. In open session, all the members show up when we have the star witness there. Before the witness gets to utter one word every member of the committee reads a ten-minute opening statement; the witness sits there for an hour, hour and a half. When the television lights go off and the press people start getting up for coffee, then a lot of the members start leaving. Some don't even stay that long. The hit-and-run operators give their statements and run out to catch the camera at some other meeting.

I haven't talked about the House at all, because it's a different group. There are more members there, a lot of outstanding members, who if they were in the Senate would do great things. But there are only a hundred senators, and I think the media gravitates to smaller groups. That's a natural thing, and you ought to continue it.

One last point. Many times we have a role to play, and you don't have that role to play: We may not wholly agree with the administration, any administration, but because of our positions we find it necessary to carry water for them. I'm not so certain we shouldn't do that. It's all right to be independent, but sometimes you have to be part of the team too.

QUESTIONS

CAROLE SIMPSON (Washington correspondent, ABC News): Senator Dole, do senators on the whole consider television more important than print?

MR. DOLE: I had that in the speech, but I looked around and saw some writing press and dropped it. The answer is yes. You run a mile for a camera, but you won't go half that far for a little print story.

MS. SIMPSON: Why is that? Just the number of people being reached?

MR. DOLE: The number of people who may be watching television. That doesn't mean that the others aren't very important, but there's something about being on television. That's why some people hang around the press gallery. A lot of members are up there wanting to know if anybody wants to talk to them.

ALBERT HUNT (Washington bureau chief, *Wall Street Journal*): What's the difference between the way the national press covers you and the way your home-state press covers you?

MR. DOLE: I was out in Hiawatha, Kansas, last week, participating in the dedication of a sheltered workshop. This one local press guy was very upset. The Indian reservation close by won't let him in to cover meetings, and he said I haven't solved his problem for him. So they are much tougher at a local level, because they get into very specific things that affect that area. They expect you to know the answer to something about a HUD grant or some little provision in the agriculture act or some tax change. Generally, I think, the national press recognizes that we may know a lot about the general subject matter but we are not expected to know every single detail.

ROGER MUDD (Washington correspondent, NBC News): Senator, in the interesting lines you drew between the efficiency and speed with which you could operate behind closed doors versus the openness of letting people in, where do you come down?

MR. DOLE: I think that all decisions ought to be made in a public session, but I believe we ought to be able to caucus. We caucused a lot on the tax reform bill last year. I'd go off with the Republican members and Russell Long would go off with the Democrats, and then we'd go back and forth negotiating. It seemed to me in a public session we couldn't make every decision.

Lobbyists are very important; they have a right to be there, to petition Congress, to have their views reflected. But in the old days—not too old, either—I used to watch lobbyists send notes up to senators. Somebody would start a little coughing fit and go out in the hallway to pick up another amendment. Some members were like vacuum cleaners; they ended up with ten amendments to offer. You never were going to finish the bill.

So I would come down to a public session everywhere, except we should have the right to separate ourselves and caucus as Republicans and Democrats.

JACQUELINE ADAMS (Capitol Hill correspondent, CBS News): Do you really think that, if more stories about the deficit appeared on the evening news, you would have the political will to do something about it?

MR. DOLE: I know it's a problem, particularly for the electronic media, but if the deficit could be translated into what it means to people—in terms of higher interest rates, higher mortgage payments—then such a message would be very helpful. Realtors are telling us that mortgage rates are about 13.5 percent nationwide average, and 14 percent is the barrier. You don't have any sales after that. They are scared to death.

ADAM CLYMER (assistant to the executive editor, *New York Times*): Senator, we polled before the last two tax cuts took effect in June of last year and June of this year, and we got resounding majorities for the proposition: "Would you give up this tax cut that's going to take effect next month if it would reduce the deficit?" And then there are half-hearted efforts to cut back the tax cut, or to produce other increases. You folks get paid $70,000 a year to make difficult decisions. Aren't you asking us to provide the courage to the Congress?

MR. DOLE: I don't know whether it's courage. At least give us a little help explaining what it is. Put in the story what the deficits are, where they are going, what it means. For instance, low-income people will particularly suffer from all this neglect of the deficit. There are things we can do on the deficit, on the revenue side and the spending side, that will not impact low-income America, not food stamps or Medicaid.

Maybe we are asking the press to give us courage, but I don't think so. What we really want is the American people to understand how bad it is, despite all the good economic news—and there is a lot of good news. We want the recovery to last. One way to make it last is to take some action now.

8

FINDINGS AND RECOMMENDATIONS
A Summation

PARTICIPANTS

Dennis A. Britton (moderator), deputy managing editor, *Los Angeles Times*
Jonathan Moore (moderator), director, Institute of Politics, Harvard University
Jacqueline Adams, Capitol Hill correspondent, CBS News
William H. Cable, partner, Williams & Jensen; former deputy assistant to President Carter for congressional liaison
Adam Clymer, assistant to the executive editor, *New York Times*
John C. Culver, former senator, D-Iowa
Paul Duke, moderator, *Washington Week in Review*
Christopher F. Edley, Jr., assistant professor, Harvard Law School; former aide to President Carter
Charles D. Ferris, attorney, Mintz, Levin, Cohn, Ferris, Glovsky & Popeo; former general counsel, Senate Democratic Policy Committee; former chairman, Federal Communications Commission
Bill Frenzel, member of Congress, R-Minnesota
James P. Gannon, editor, *Des Moines Register*
Roy M. Goodman, New York state senator (R)
Stephen H. Hess, senior fellow, Brookings Institution; author, *The Washington Reporters*
Albert R. Hunt, Washington bureau chief, *Wall Street Journal*
James McCartney, national correspondent, Knight-Ridder Newspapers
Charles McDowell, Washington columnist, *Richmond Times-Dispatch*

Joan McKinney, Washington correspondent, *Baton Rouge Morning Advocate and States Times*

John K. Meagher, vice-president for government relations, LTV Corporation; former staff minority counsel for Committee on Ways and Means

Norman C. Miller, national editor, *Los Angeles Times*

Roger Mudd, Washington correspondent, NBC News

David R. Obey, member of Congress, D-Wisconsin

Norman J. Ornstein, visiting scholar, American Enterprise Institute; editor, *Congress in Change*

Leo Rennert, Washington bureau chief, McClatchy Newspapers of California

Carole Simpson, Washington correspondent, ABC News

Frank Stanton, president emeritus, CBS Inc.

Pete Wilson, senator, R-California

JONATHAN MOORE: The idea here is not to force rigid closure on prescriptions. We will not, for instance, have votes or negotiations on language. We do want some useful focus and general consensus on what we've identified and what, if anything, might be done about it.

Two teams—one from the Congress side and one from the media side—met last night to compile some basic findings and recommendations. The team captains, Al Hunt for the media team and Charlie Ferris for the Congress team, will report on those shortly, and we'll discuss them. Then we'll open it up for additional points.

MEDIA FINDINGS AND RECOMMENDATIONS

ALBERT R. HUNT: Let me quickly run through our findings, and then focus on the recommendations.

The media are important. If they weren't, we wouldn't be here. They are important both as a conduit for information from Congress, and as an independent source of information and explanation.

Coverage, particularly by print, has improved in recent years. But much of the coverage still is simplistic and negative, and it focuses on conflict and confrontation. Conflict and confrontation are news, and we do a pretty good job of covering that, but sometimes we don't do nearly the job we should on process and issues.

There was also some concern that the Senate is still emphasized over the House, though we basically felt that the situation has changed.

Much of our discussion focused on the problems of television.

Picking up on the suggestions that both Chuck Jones and Roger Mudd offered, we think that different standards ought to be developed for evaluating television's performance.

We did not agree that there's a problem of access. Several people raised that, but I think most people who cover Congress would agree that if there's any problem, it's choosing among a whole lot of people who are dying to talk.

Let me turn to the recommendations.

The one we spent the most time discussing, and which we think is the most important and interesting, was suggested by Roger Mudd. When the majority and the minority leadership of the House and Senate decide that an issue is important enough for a great national debate, we urge that the Congress make arrangements to provide for such a debate and make it available to television, to air in prime time. In our discussion we envisioned this as occurring once or twice a year, for issues ranging from Central America to the Middle East to tax policies. We felt that it might provide some very interesting debate.

We also recommend televising the Senate.

We also urge that reporters spend more time writing about the connection between a member at home and a member in Washington.

We encourage all news organizations to run roll-call votes by their local members. It was noted by Jim Gannon and others that the members often don't like that, but we think it's the responsibility of a newspaper to let constituents know how their member voted.

Particularly in the Senate, we urge that there be more debate. It really has declined markedly in recent years.

We encourage newspapers and television to report more on one another's coverage.

Finally, in what I think was really a bold move, we decided that journalists should be better educated.

PRIME-TIME CONGRESSIONAL DEBATES

JOHN C. CULVER: Your suggestion about televised debates is very interesting and potentially useful. But I wonder how realistic it is, how it could be organized consistent with Senate rules and procedures.

We have unlimited debate. You can do anything with unanimous consent, but with a hundred members jockeying for those three hours I wonder how you do it without allocating two or three minutes each—and that's no debate. I wonder how you could get the quality of exercise you're seeking for public education. It seems to me that's a pretty formidable consideration.

ROGER MUDD: The purpose of the suggestion was to try to break out of the dilemma that you are in and we are in, particularly on commercial television where, like it or not, the quality has declined with the increase in competition. Every minute now is so expensive that there aren't any minutes left to televise long sessions. There are alternative outlets, C-SPAN and PBS, but the major audience is still with the commercial networks.

The evening news doesn't appear likely to get longer in the foreseeable future. It looks like it's locked in for thirty minutes for another five or ten years. Even if it goes to an hour, the question is what we would do with that hour. Instead of nine stories, would we just have eighteen stories? I'm not very hopeful that an hour broadcast would improve the situation; there would always be the minute-and-a-half, short, snappy piece.

So the suggestion is that the minority and majority leadership in both the House and the Senate agree occasionally, when a major issue is of national importance, to adopt a set of rules that would produce a meaningful debate. It would require the House and Senate to modify their rules, just as it would require us to rearrange our evening schedule. You could not have unlimited debate; it would not be fair in the House to have the one-minute rule. The leadership would have to work it out ahead of time. It would in effect produce a televised debate, as the Canadians do at noon every day.

It could be that the networks could rotate, taking turns. The first debate, say on Grenada, would be ABC's. The next time a major issue was declared, it would be CBS's turn. It seems to me the demand from the public would force the networks to carry it.

MR. CULVER: I think it could be very valuable, but it's hard to envision how the leadership might construct such an arrangement. You'd need to select maybe ten spokesmen out of your membership on either side. You'll pick the ten guys running for reelection; that's going to be all politics. Then you're going to have to have set speeches because nobody wants to jump in cold turkey. The only valuable debate is when you have a hard-hitting exchange where tough questions are asked. The Senate today doesn't debate at all. They are not used to that kind of thing.

MR. MUDD: There's no pressure on them to do it.

MR. CULVER: No particular pressure. From a leadership point of view, I think it would be very tough to get the spontaneity and integrity in that kind of exchange of which you get flashes during floor debate.

DAVID R. OBEY: What would be your objection to summarizing and excerpting two or three hours of debate that has already occurred, so that it would be more natural rather than staged for the national audience?

MR. MUDD: I'm not sure there would be an objection. There would be the problem of who would do the excerpting and whether you would be pleased with our editing, and also the whole question of when it should be aired. That's a possible avenue, but if it was a live broadcast there would not be those nettlesome problems.

MR. OBEY: If you had that sort of coverage, I would trust your people's news judgment a hell of a lot more than I would our ability to manufacture a real debate as opposed to a dog and pony show.

MR. HUNT: David, I think the point goes to your complaints about the tax issue of 1981. Every now and then issues are so important, let's air them. By periodically setting aside that three hours at night, you really dramatize an issue. It may be that the leadership won't perform very well, but at least provide that opportunity.

PETE WILSON: If there is going to be televising of the Senate floor proceedings, which I think there will be, it is going to force a change in the rules. The chief change is going to be that there will no longer be unlimited debate. There simply can't be.

But that is entirely due. It will result in a good deal more debate than currently occurs. There's debate now, but it's very sporadic, very hit or miss, because most of the time you have an empty chamber. You look up and see the galleries utterly bewildered, wondering what in hell is going on with someone making an impassioned speech to an empty chamber. It is only rarely that something brings people to the floor.

We are not going to determine this morning how these debates will happen, but they should be encouraged. What you're going to have to do is allow the leadership on both sides to stage the debate, and if they stage a dull debate, that's their tough luck. But I don't think you want to be editing, because you will undoubtedly be criticized. If you simply have live coverage of what is offered, you can't be criticized.

THE ECONOMICS OF NETWORK TELEVISION

CHARLES D. FERRIS: This is academic, because the commercial networks are in the business of making money. Dr. Stanton, what would be the networks' attitude be to giving up three hours in prime time twice a year for something of this nature?

FRANK STANTON: One of the advantages of being retired is that you can talk without being held responsible. I think Roger has come upon a very interesting idea. But one of the problems that the networks will face is the same problem they face concerning hour-long news: If Wichita and Fort Wayne aren't going to carry it, then it dies with the company-owned stations. You would have one-hour news today were it not for the affiliates, but there is no way that we can push the button and get coast-to-coast coverage.

The first time up I would think it would have acceptance by one of the networks. It will not get much audience, and the affiliates the next time up are going to be very difficult to persuade. But you'll never find out unless you try. It's a fascinating approach.

ADAM CLYMER: Two quick thoughts.

I'm not sure there wouldn't be an audience. Our poll indicated that 46 percent of adult Americans listened to President Reagan Thursday night [October 27, 1983]. Now, that was an extraordinary subject [Grenada], but you're talking about debates on extraordinary subjects.

Second, if the television networks want to shame the Senate into letting cameras in, they could air hour-long excerpts of house debates. The House does debate, and it isn't reading set speeches; they argue with one another. When there is a hot issue they bring it to the floor. It's there from the House television system, and network television could make an hour out of it if they wanted to. If the issue was critical enough, the Fort Wayne station that dumped it would be hearing from the people in Fort Wayne. Obviously, if you tried to do it once a week they wouldn't, but if you did it a couple of times a year you could get away with it.

NORMAN J. ORNSTEIN: I would endorse this notion for a variety of reasons. If there were an evening debate on Grenada right now in the Senate, I think it would be carried by the networks. Maybe not for three hours; one hour might be better, and it would get a better audience.

The Senate rules could be changed to provide for a special session with special rules, maybe operating under the five-minute rule as the House does. It would be easy to devise a set of rules that would limit the degree of staging.

Realistically speaking, the House isn't going to be covered by television in that fashion, as it isn't now, because it's the House.

They had a wonderful debate on Lebanon, stirring and interesting, but it wasn't covered on prime time. The Senate would be.

MR. CULVER: Could you elaborate on how easy it would be to design those rules? Say you've got a five-minute rule. How about, "Would the gentleman yield for a question?"

MR. ORNSTEIN: I would certainly have provisions, as the House does, for yielding. And I hope there would be a lot of that.

MR. CULVER: You'll give up part of your five minutes of prime time to somebody else?

MR. ORNSTEIN: Either that or say, "Shut up, I won't yield," and look like a fool. Look at the House now. They get debate.

WILLIAM H. CABLE: Isn't there already a mechanism to do this without changing the rules? Take the debate into committee, where there isn't the unlimited debate problem in the Senate, where there is already television allowed in the Senate and House. Produce something there for television as an experiment, without having to force the issue of changing the House or Senate rules. I think everybody would agree that you get better debate in Senate committees than you do on the floor. And you have a mechanism to try something creative and novel like that, without having to change the rules.

DR. STANTON: I hope that in whatever language finally comes out somebody puts in a footnote to protect the broadcasters from Section 315 problems. [Section 315 requires equal airtime opportunities for candidates.] In the House you're going to have everybody running for reelection, and in the Senate you're going to have a third of them running. If it's a news event we are out from under 315, but some guy will come out and start talking about it. So I'd nail that down.

JAMES McCARTNEY: I'm not sure this is as difficult a problem as some here seem to think. There have been real news events and real drama in the Senate. The final debate on the AWACs question—it was a hot subject and there was real debate. The advantage of the Senate over a committee is, you get all the stars with personalities. Unusual as it may seem, there really can be intelligent debate in the Senate. The capability is there; you've just got to force them to do it publicly.

PAUL DUKE: What I see as the real problem here is that instead of real debate you'll get a staged debate. It's a very good idea in principle, but the great need is to get the Senate opened up completely to television. Then television itself can decide what to put on and when to put it on.

MR. HUNT: Before the House Judiciary Committee met on impeachment, that's what everybody said: "You're going to get a staged debate; they'll all have prepared remarks, and it will be dreadful." In fact, that was one of the most dramatic events in any of our lives. You underestimate the ability of people to rise to the occasion.

MR. DUKE: That went on day after day, not just three hours.

PRINTING ROLL-CALL VOTES

LEO RENNERT: On printing roll-call votes, just a small modification. That can take two formats, one very good and one totally useless. Totally useless is to wrap them up on the weekend and put them near the classifieds, so the professors and other addicts read them. The good way to do it is to incorporate the roll call with the story. If the House votes to cut off aid to Nicaragua, put it in the story. The wires provide roll calls now; it's very easy.

DENNIS BRITTON: What about doing it both ways?

MR. RENNERT: The first way is a cop-out, a waste.

JAMES P. GANNON: We do it both ways in the *Register*. When there's an important vote, we incorporate it in the story. Every weekend we report every roll-call vote. It's not in the classified ads, but it is in little agate type. But people read that thing. They clip it out. I think, John, you know that people read it.

MR. CULVER: Unfortunately.

MR. OBEY: I would like to weigh in on Leo's side. When people in my district read the story and they don't like what the House did, they are madder than hell. They have no idea how I voted. So by far the most valuable way is to run it in the story, so that people have some idea how their guy voted the only time they will be reading about that event.

CROSS-MEDIA CRITICISM

CAROLE SIMPSON: I have a question about media criticizing one another. What does that mean? ABC will criticize the *New York Times*?

MR. HUNT: For instance, there's been a lot of discussion up here of the *60 Minutes* piece done recently on Congress. It might not be a bad idea for a newspaper to go look at that and do a piece.

CBS News did a good piece on a picture that ran on the front page of the *Washington Post* and other papers, of George Shultz putting his hand over his face when Paul X. Kelley [Marine Commandant] was confusing Vietnam and Lebanon. The only problem was, George Shultz had put his hand over his face ten seconds before Kelley said that. That kind of critique of one another is a good idea, and I would encourage more of that.

CONGRESS FINDINGS AND RECOMMENDATIONS

MR. FERRIS: Maybe there should have been more discussion that the relationship between Congress and the media is not adversarial enough, because independently we both came to very similar conclusions about what should be done to improve the relationship.

It was felt in our group that both institutions have tremendous limitations. The Congress and the media are both made up of human beings who operate under artificially imposed restraints and as a result, err. The news media have deadlines that force them to reach factual conclusions without being able to get all the information.

We also believe it is important to distinguish between the various media—national, regional, and local; newspapers, radio, and television; and local as opposed to network television.

There was a very evident sentiment in our group about national versus local reporters. You're much more comfortable dealing with your local reporter; you know him, you know where he's coming from. Nobody reads the national reporter's work product back home anyway. Dealing with the national media is more to communicate with or to influence your peers in the Congress or the other branches of government, than with your constituency. So dealing with a national reporter is perceived by some as nothing better than a no-win situation, but can be a significant-loss situation.

In addition, we are troubled by the pettiness of media coverage, the overemphasis on scandals, trivia, superficiality, and the horse race.

Stories also often fail to recognize the fact that Capitol Hill is a bottom-line organization, that no decision is made until it's all over. Therefore, Congress looks like a zoo in comparison to the executive branch, which has such discipline and speaks with such clarity. The Congress institutionally looks like a fool. However, these are aspects of media coverage that contribute to—but are not solely responsible for—the negative attitude toward Congress as an institution.

In our recommendations, we believe that the media should be permitted to cover almost any process they want to cover on Capitol Hill. Included in that is television coverage.

We also believe that reporters should seek out the major players who have special knowledge. We had some suspicions that if your name is Ted Kennedy [senator, D-Massachusetts] or half a dozen others on Capitol Hill, you're going to get on the front page above the fold regardless of what the story is. But there are other people who know an awful lot about selected issues and who might if asked make a significant contribution. It was perceived that this might be directed more at the producer or the editor back home. But it is a perceived problem—the role of personality in dictating coverage of an issue. There was strongly expressed sentiment on our committee that reporters should be more experienced and better informed, and that the media should try to reduce the turnover in congressional reporters, in order to develop a sense of trust.

There was also a sentiment expressed with respect to the emphasis in the media to report about perks. The media should apply the same set of standards to Congress, the executive branch, businesses, and themselves.

Finally, there was interest in the producers of the evening news programs. Who are they? What are their value systems? There was greater comfort with editors of newspapers, apparently because they were known. I think it manifests again the basic suspicion about whether there is a secret agenda.

OPENING CONGRESS UP

JACQUELINE ADAMS: I'm troubled by the first recommendation, that the media be able to cover "almost" any process on the Hill. Who decides?

MR. FERRIS: It would be the Congress that would decide.

MS. ADAMS: But Ways and Means has closed meetings so people don't posture for the press when forming tax policies.

MR. FERRIS: In the Senate they have had secret sessions about four times in the past two decades. They claim they are going to talk about very sensitive national security matters. They exclude all staff and go into session. Nothing very dramatic or very secret takes place, but everyone comes because they expect something important might take place.

MS. ADAMS: That's quite different from a meeting where the members are trying to decide on a tax increase.

JOAN McKINNEY: It relates to the media's finding that Congress is so very accessible. In our discussions we skimmed over what some people see as a trend, especially in the tax-writing committees, to go behind closed doors.

MR. MUDD: Would "almost" exclude coverage of the mark-up?

MR. FERRIS: No. But under the recently revised rules of the

Senate, as I remember them, a majority vote is required to close a session, whereas before it was just by the dictate of the chairman. The sentiment in our committee is to urge a policy of maximum coverage and to exclude only when there is a significant issue of national security.

BILL FRENZEL: I will speak for the open convenant secretly arrived at. There are going to be times when units of Congress will want to close the doors, and you in the press are going to be very disappointed. You're going to think the republic has fallen and the Constitution has shattered. But that is going to happen, sometimes for good reasons and sometimes for bad reasons. You're not going to convince us it is not better to operate that way occasionally. And we probably can't convince you that one of the stories you're very proud of was a piece of junk.

JOHN K. MEAGHER: Since I've changed incarnations I'm concerned about this from a different perspective. I think the trend is to close hearings, particularly tax hearings. Rostenkowski always wants to close things. When they go into a caucus, they essentially mark up the bill and then go out in public. They call for the vote and it's over; there really isn't any debate. Guys like Bill Frenzel tend to vote against closing, but what they always do is arrange enough votes to close it and let the guys who have to vote that way off the hook. They have to do that from time to time, but it's not a great trend.

The other thing that's important to mention is the speed with which this is done. Senator Dole essentially is proposing a major change in the law in forty-eight hours. Nobody is going to know what happened, including the people who vote on it. As Russell Long [senator, D-Louisiana] said, you don't have to know what you're voting on, just vote. That's a problem for all of us. You can't cover that. You have no notion what's involved, the ramifications. All of a sudden, after forty-eight hours of closed-door sessions, $110 billion is changed in the budget of this country.

BRINGING TELEVISION PRODUCERS TO CONGRESS

MR. DUKE: I'd like to say a few words about the point that it would be helpful for producers of the evening news to visit the Hill. The producers are the real decision-makers most of the time, but I think it would also be very helpful to introduce news executives to the legislative process. All too often they don't know what it is.

MS. SIMPSON: Congress should understand better how television news functions, too. There's a lot of criticism of network television. I don't think a lot of members of Congress understand what we do, and that we can often in a minute and a half get in a great deal of information. It would be very helpful if you understood how a story gets from a hearing to the evening news, and our constraints.

DR. STANTON: I think the recommendation is too narrowly focused. Most affiliates around the country are now carrying, I would estimate, four hours of news a day. I'm not counting the all-night news, just the morning news, the late-afternoon news, the evening news, and the late evening news. There's an enormous opportunity to get a lot of coverage in those spots. The producers of all broadcast news ought to be given attention on this point, not just the evening news.

You've also got something else out there that you ought to pay attention to: cable. We have completely ignored it here. I'd like to ignore it too, but we have to be realistic. The technology that's right around the corner is going to open up an enormous amount of time. Everybody needs, not to look back at what we have been doing, but to think in terms of the opportunities that are out there.

Throughout the discussions, you also neglected one other means of the transfer of information, the way that an enormous amount of news is moved in this country: radio. You have a captive audience on the car radio. An enormous number of people use that for their news. National Public Radio's morning and late-afternoon news are two of the best news programs on anybody's airwaves.

EDUCATING HOME-STATE REPORTERS

MR. CULVER: One problem is the quality of state coverage of candidates seeking congressional or senatorial office. I'm thinking of dailies, in cities of fifty- or sixty-thousand population, that have no Washington bureau at all, or possibly a stringer who has never talked to the person who will cover you in the state.

Perhaps state news associations, broadcast associations, or newspapers could organize seminars. The two candidates could submit the four issues that they feel are central to the campaign. Informational, educational seminars of a totally nonpartisan nature—the candidates wouldn't be there—could be arranged for the reporters who cover the campaign. It would develop greater sophistication, background, and perspective on those subjects.

That's a very important aspect. It's life or death to the members and the candidates, how effectively they and their positions are being filtered through to the electorate.

MR. BRITTON: Bill Frenzel, do you have any reaction to that?

MR. FRENZEL: No. I live and work in blissful anonymity, and I love it. I don't have those kinds of problems. John runs statewide. In a congressional district one can know the media representatives without too much difficulty.

MUCH ADO ABOUT NOTHING

MR. CLYMER: One of the things that bothers me about Congress and the media, and it's something that we do jointly, is sometimes we pay far too much attention to Congress. Congress debates something day after day. It leads papers, including mine, day after day. And it isn't nearly as much of an issue as it's said to be.

For example, the public works jobs bill of last winter wasn't going to solve unemployment, nor was it going to bust an already terribly red-inked budget, yet you had extremely passionate arguments on both sides. We did a story about four months later, and we found about one state in which it had produced more than a thousand jobs. We sometimes get caught up in an issue which both Congress and the press think is symbolic of some grave national problem like unemployment, and we all treat it as bigger than it is.

MEDIA AND CONGRESS AS CO-CONSPIRATORS

CHRISTOPHER F. EDLEY, JR.: I want to say a couple of general words as an outsider. My overwhelming impression from listening to you folks is that the much-vaunted adversarial relationship between the media and the Congress really is not there. I am struck by the number of areas of agreement, the number of areas where it seems you have a common interest. It looks like a situation akin to regulatory capture. In many respects I sense a conspiracy between the media and the Congress, a conspiracy about what constitutes news, about what kinds of questions are going to be asked. I'm not convinced that the standard retort—that we have good journalism so we don't have any problems—is really sufficient.

I don't think we came to grips enough with what is newsworthy and who has responsibility for clarifying issues. As a voter and a reader, I want to know a lot more about banality, about ignorance, about ducking issues, than the media is giving me. There's too much tendency to say it's business as usual, not worth reporting. But you report a lot of things that are boring day after day. I'm not sure that your collective sense of what is newsworthy is necessarily in the best interests of the public.

My second point is about professionalism and expertise. Lawyers are perhaps better than any other professional group at insisting that if you're smart, you can handle just about any problem that walks in the door. It's obviously very common in journalism too. But as a reader, as a consumer of news, I am simply not satisfied with that. I have some friends in journalism who are very smart, but I simply don't believe that they can go from covering a complicated story at Health and Human Services on Tuesday to a complicated story in the Finance Committee on Wednesday, and do anything but a half-assed job.

I don't think readers are being served as well as we would like, and I wish I had heard some discussions about ways to break out of the conventional assumptions.

NORMAN C. MILLER: Picking up on that, I'm struck by the fact that the tone of the findings and recommendations on both sides implies that the press should be Congress's buddy, that our role is to make them look good. I don't think that's our role at all. The Congress doesn't belong to the members.

MR. FERRIS: The sentiment that came across in our group was not that it's the mission of the press to make the Congress look good, but neither is it to make the Congress look bad. The sense of the group was that somehow in the dynamic of getting into the paper, there is an incentive to make someone look bad. If you have a carcass to hang you're going to get better placement of your by-line.

MR. FRENZEL: We don't need to be written up. We just don't want you to play [John] LeBoutillier [former member of Congress, R-New York] in every article, and we think that you often do.

CHARLES McDOWELL: This doesn't need saying, but I'm going to ride back more comfortably if I say it. I was moved by Chris Edley's remarks. I hope the press is good at self-criticism, and I know how wholesome Congress's attention to our problems is. But I hope the context in which this is set forth is that of an adversarial relationship. Bumbling and idiotic as we must be, we represent the damn people—so do they—and our job is to poke at these very strong, very powerful people. Seminars, all getting together to make reporters understand it better, is fine—within the context that these are two very important, adversarial organizations.

EXPERTISE BY SUBSCRIPTION

STEPHEN H. HESS: I want to add one area we left out, just as Dr. Stanton talked about cable and radio, and it may help in response to Chris Edley too: the trade press, specialized publications. For far less than the cost of one additional reporter, a bureau could buy into hundreds of experts by selectively subscribing to specialized publications and circulating them among the staff. They could pick up many stories that would otherwise be unknown to them, stories with considerable ramifications, particularly consumer ramifications. So I suggest one way to fill the gap of knowledge that every generalist reporter has is to consider the usefulness of colleagues whose names you probably don't know.

OBJECTIVE, NOT ADVERSARIAL

ROY M. GOODMAN: I'd like to make two brief observations.

First, I take very vigorous exception to the notion that it is the press's mission to be adversarial. Their sacred mission is to be objective—to be intensely expository about everything. The press must provide illumination of the democratic process in a free society. For the press to be solely adversarial carries with it the potential danger of driving the politicians out of politics, forcing them to retreat from public life. If all the press does is poke holes in public officials, why should they continue to be politicians? Surely government pay is insufficient incentive.

Second, I favor televising public meetings and opening up the political process as much as possible. Clearly, caucuses have got to be excluded because they represent the internal deliberations of a party. Whether mark-ups should be included is debatable.

I certainly favor televising the plenary sessions of the Senate. On cable now you can observe the House of Representatives. There's substantial value in watching that parade of people go to the microphone in the well of the House. We should push very hard for getting the Senate on television wherever it can reasonably be done.

APPENDIX

Major Issues in Congress-Media Relations: A Topical Outline
by Stephen Bates

I. CENTRAL THEMES

    A. The special character and challenge of media coverage of Congress; how and how well it is done; what its consequences might be.

    B. Congress as a cohesive national institution, pursuing its constitutional roles, versus Congress as a collection of individual actors, characterized overall by fragmented activity and decentralized authority.

    C. The influence of media coverage of Congress on the performance of members as national legislators versus as "district errand boys."

    D. The difference in character, motivation, and impact of national versus local coverage of Congress and its members.

    E. The goals of congressional news; how they might be better pursued by both sides.

II. OVERVIEW OF COVERAGE

    A. *Quantity*

        1. Congress versus president

        Most studies agree that the White House receives more coverage than Congress. A 1976 analysis of Chicago newspapers found that 37 percent of stories concerned the president; 27 percent concerned Congress. In network television—the most relied-upon news medium—the discrepancy was more dramatic, 47 percent to 24 percent. [Graber 193-4] (One study gives Congress a slight edge over the president; however, it was conducted while the House was preparing for impeachment hearings, and thus may represent an exceptional period. [Miller (b)])

Further, presidential dominance has increased over time. In a study of newspapers from 1835 to 1957, Cornwell found that "Presidential news, and by inference the public's image of the Presidency and its relative governmental importance, has increased markedly and more or less steadily in this century, particularly since World War I." [283] Using the same methodology, Balutis studied newspapers for the years 1958 to 1974. The increase in presidential news coverage continued, he found. "On the other hand, the pattern in congressional news has been one of steady decline, both in absolute terms and relative to news about the President." [514]

2. Senate versus House

Of congressional coverage in several major newspapers in 1973-4, Miller found that "47 percent were about Senate activities, 37 percent about House activities, and the remainder about joint committees and undifferentiated activities. . . ." [Miller (b) 461] In an interview with Miller, Eileen Shanahan of the *New York Times* explained: "The House is not so much undercovered as underplayed. It's very hard to get a story about representatives on Page 1 because our editors don't know their names. . . . Every editor knows who Muskie and Scott are. They assume their readers do too. Names make the news. That's an oversimplification. But there's something to it." [462]

In network news coverage, the contrast is again more dramatic: nearly a two-to-one advantage for the Senate, according to Robinson and Appel. [410]

Reasons may include the facts that the Senate has fewer members, that it deals more with international issues, and that it contains more presidential aspirants courting the national media.

B. *Tone*

Miller et al. studied 10 front pages from each of 94 newspapers from the year 1974. They report that, of all political coverage, 63 percent is neutral in tone, 31 percent is negative, and 6 percent is positive. In contrast, 42 percent of congressional coverage is negative—exceeded only by the negative coverage accorded political parties. The full findings:

United States	10 percent
Supreme Court	25
State, local gov't	34
President Ford	38
The administration	40
Congress	42
Political parties	70 [71, fig.2]

Television seems even more negative. Robinson argues that television has an anti-institutional tone in general, "with one essential message: none of our national policies work, none of our institutions respond, none of our political organizations succeed." [Robinson (a) 429] Robinson and Appel found that 86 percent of congressional stories on television were neutral, but *all* non-neutral coverage was negative. [412]

C. *Content*

Miller argues that the president is covered automatically; Congress is covered only by virtue of its association with existing, newsworthy topics. "Unlike Congress, the President tended to have the ability to establish topics as newsworthy by virtue of his association with them. When this happened, Congress was covered only to the extent that it differed from the President, added new information or took definitive action." [Miller (b) 465] Eileen Shanahan agreed: "Nobody covers the legislative process. We do only insofar as we cover topics that are substantially or politically important. Coverage of Congress is almost a byproduct of topic coverage." [Ibid. 463]

Edward Jay Epstein posits a different, though not contradictory, argument concerning television. Television, he finds, shows Congress principally in its investigative role. "[T]he legislative process itself—the passing of laws and approval of appropriations—was almost completely neglected."

He suggests two explanations: that cameras were permitted in hearings but not on the floor (at the time); and that television is hungry for confrontation and drama. [251] Robinson and Appel provide evidence for Epstein's assertion. Over a third of congressional coverage, they found, concerns committee action. Further, "Almost 60 percent of the items coded as committee action were testimony—usually vivid testimony—before congressional committees." [411]

III. INHERENT DIFFICULTIES IN MEDIA COVERAGE OF CONGRESS

    A. The complexity of Congress, as an institution, makes it difficult to cover. Facets of complexity:

1. Over time. No bill reaches a vote without months or years of work by a variety of actors in Congress and elsewhere.
2. In space. Committees, subcommittees, caucuses all meet simultaneously.
3. Procedurally. E.g., the manner in which the House Rules Committee shapes legislation by controlling the amending process; the complex but often inconclusive parliamentary maneuvering that may surround votes.
4. In motives. Why a member votes as he did—lobbying, district interests or pressure, ideology, owed favors.
5. Substantively. Issues often are more complex, surrounded by more considerations, with more groups who stand to gain or to lose.
6. In authority. Leadership clout has declined in the past decade; unlike the White House, nobody's in charge. There is a mix of shared and competing authority.

B. The showhorse versus workhorse point. Many of the institution's major players won't talk, or won't talk freely; members who court the media are sometimes less relevant to internal processes.

C. At the same time, constraints exist on the media: limited manpower; limited space/time for political news in general and congressional news in particular; the need to appeal to a heterogeneous audience with varying levels of attentiveness and prior knowledge.

Among the issues related to limited resources: Can we expect adequate congressional coverage from papers that are too small to have their own Washington bureaus? To what extent do the newspaper chains' bureaus and the wire services respond to the needs of individual papers for congressional coverage? To what extent must the local paper or broadcast outlet ultimately rely on members themselves to supply news about the institution? Is it desirable (or even feasible) for news organizations to cover the member's Washington performance in terms of district and state politics? Can the national press organs afford to do anything but cover the latest-breaking issues as seen through the eyes of the leadership? Does this encourage coverage that focuses on senators at the expense of representatives? Do limited resources encourage coverage that focuses on individuals, rather than on processes and institutions?

D. National/local media: Different media have different degrees of access to members.
1. The national media are often courted by senators. As noted previously, senators are judged more newsworthy

than representatives. Further, their states, unlike representatives' districts, sometimes hold a significant share of a national medium's audience. Also, senators have presidential ambitions more frequently, or more nakedly, than representatives.

2. Representatives, conversely, sometimes avoid the national press. They fear that a reporter may push them into a corner, forcing them to announce a position or plan before they're ready, or to lie about it. Many see no positive advantage in displaying their views before a national audience, or at least no advantage adequate to offset the attendant risks. On the House side, thus, the national media may have trouble getting as complete a story as on the Senate side.

3. Members face special challenges in trying to gain coverage in the national media. Les Aspin has distinguished between a source story—news because of who says it—and an information story—news because of what is said. The member can usually get coverage at home whenever he wants (source news), but he needs something big to break into the national press (information news). The latter would include more information, better information, information ahead of others, or demonstrated expertise.

4. Local media are usually courted by all members, who want to communicate with their constituents.

5. However, local media may have trouble gaining access to members from other states or districts.

6. Also, in dealing with members, local media may lack the expertise that comes from specialization and experience.

IV. WHAT EACH SIDE WANTS FROM THE OTHER

A. *Media*

Broadly: good stories, which will receive prominent play and attract attention. The reporter will enjoy his work; peers will admire him; he will get Pulitzers, Niemans, book contracts, invitations to Sunday morning panel shows, better jobs, and higher salaries.

1. General elements of the news

    a. Conflict, confrontation. Tendency to shape complex issues with many sides as bipolar—and frequently as good guys versus bad guys, especially on television. At the systemic level, tendency to shape major policy battles (e.g., Lebanon and the War Powers Act) almost exclusively as White House versus Congress.

b. Simplicity, brevity. In part a preference for events over process, for process over down-the-road results, for action over deliberation.

c. Personalities. Combined with the desire for conflict and confrontation, this means that policy battles are frequently depicted as individual battles. As James Verdier writes: "Back in the old days (pre-1970s), Congress was run in a way that played to the media's strength: a few senior people dominated the place, so the media's emphasis on personalities and simplifying issues did a good job of capturing reality. With the growing decentralization of the 1970s, that approach no longer works. The multiple players on every issue and the complicated institutional cross-currents are much harder to capture and convey."

d. Secrets. Regardless of their intrinsic value, secrets generally make bigger news than ordinary announcements. J. William Fulbright has written that a Foreign Relations Committee staff member "suggested that the committee had made a mistake in holding the 1974 detente hearings in public; if they had been held in closed session and the transcripts then leaked, the press would have covered them generously." [42]

2. Spokesmen, structures, and processes that make news-gathering easier or more exciting. As George Will remarked, testifying against televising the Senate: "There is an understandable predilection on the part of journalists to think that those government procedures are best which make the craft of journalism more stimulating to practice." [U.S. Senate 41]

B. *Congress*

Broadly: an open, uncritical conduit for the members' statements and information, in order to inform/persuade voters; a reliable source of information about problems and issues, about political realities and what other players are up to, about what the public believes and wants.

1. To gain reelection. Mayhew argues that the "electoral connection" prompts members to engage in three activities: credit-claiming (taking credit for district-benefiting action, regardless of the member's actual responsibility), advertising (keeping his name before the voters), and position-taking (making statements on current problems, to an extent regardless of the member's involvement in trying to legislate solutions). In all of these, the media can play a major role.

2. To bolster the public's image of Congress as an institution. The assumption underlying this seems to be that Congress is currently misunderstood, and that more and/or better coverage would help. The quality argument concerning print has been made by Miller et al.: "[T]he presentation of news in a manner that conveys a high degree of political conflict or criticism leads to a sense of distrust and inefficacy among newspaper readers." [77] Robinson has found that television causes a particularly high level of dissatisfaction concerning Congress. In a 1968 survey, people were asked whether they agreed that congressmen "lose touch with the people pretty quickly." Of white respondents, 68 percent who relied solely on television for news agreed; only 45 percent who relied primarily on other news media agreed. [Robinson (a) table 9]

   A fundamental conflict of goals seems to arise here. Members want to increase respect for their institution, but they are inevitably more interested in gaining reelection. If Congress is unpopular, then members seeking reelection have an incentive to join in the criticism. As Fenno has described it: "Members run *for* Congress by running *against* Congress. They refurbish their individual reputations as 'the best congressman in the United States' by attacking the collective reputation of the Congress of the United States." [Fenno (b) 280]

3. To inform constituents of the member's views, in order to elicit feedback. In arguing in favor of allowing television cameras in the Senate, Pat Moynihan said: "We do what we think the people we represent want, for the reason ... that we wish to be reelected in all but abnormal circumstances. The question is knowing what they want. ... [N]othing will reach as many people or produce a more representative response than being able to say what you think on television and having them watch it, because you will get back their response, and you will respond thereto. And that is in large—not entire—but in large sense, our purpose in this body." [U.S. Senate 32]

4. At the national level, as a platform for advertising the member's name and qualifications, in pursuit of higher office.

5. As a channel through which to communicate with other elites.

6. As a method of harassing enemies. Les Aspin, angry at Eddie Hebert, learned that the Army was testing poison gas on beagles. Aspin prepared a press release announc-

ing that one man, Armed Services chair Hebert, could stop the slaughter—and generated bagsful of angry mail to Hebert. Recently, Phil Gramm's office helped the Republican National Committee with releases attacking Democrats for voting against a Gramm-sponsored amendment to the International Monetary Fund which would have restricted loans to Communist countries; the releases were sent into Democratic members' districts. Similarly, congressmen may hold preplanned hearings in order to make an uncooperative executive agency, or the president's advisers, look rigid, uninformed, dictatorial.

7. As a source of information on public attitudes, opinions, and concerns.

V. PROBLEMS AND EFFECTS

A. *Media Problems with Congress*

1. Many of Congress's most newsworthy activities take place behind the scenes. Sometimes it's the selfish choice of players, who want to avoid the press; sometimes the scrutiny would hinder the process; sometimes legitimate national security arguments can be raised. Reporters generally don't like being shut out, whatever the reason.

2. Reporters frequently voice defensiveness at members' efforts to bypass the press and communicate directly with constituents. The severity of the problem is a matter of debate. Haskell and Bagdikian suggest that members' handouts are published widely and in toto at the local level. Another study argues otherwise. Examining the use of congressional press releases in a Wisconsin district, Polk et al. concluded that "office holders studied are minimally successful in mailings to weekly newspapers. Editors are not so gullible and do not passively accept Capitol Hill press releases." [546] Still, some of members' releases were published intact and unchanged—something that never happens at the national level.

3. Special problems of television. Gans has concluded that "despite the differences between the electronic and print news media, the similarities were more decisive." [xii] But some of the differences have particular relevance to congressional coverage.

    a. Television producers prefer film coverage of news.
        i. The House floor proceedings are televised, but House employees control the cameras. Part of a story may be the fact that the House chamber is nearly empty, but that can't be shown.

ii. The Senate floor has prohibited live television coverage. The networks must frequently describe goings-on while the visual is of an artist's rendering of the speaker. As a consequence, the networks frequently must try to get senators to visit the television gallery and repeat, for the cameras, the statements made on the floor. Obviously the senators can then make their statements clearer or more murky, sharper or softer.

iii. Television people feel that these restrictions limit their ability to do their jobs. The strength of television, they argue, lies in its capacity to capture a moment in a way print cannot duplicate. Congress's restrictions on television, therefore, remove the medium's strongest element.

iv. Television's need for visuals is important off the floor, too. Producers favor film footage of a relevant actor stating his position, rather than of the correspondent telling what the position is. In an institution where much information is given only on background, the need for filmed interviews can become a hindrance.

v. Finally, producers favor film that depicts action, emotion, or drama. Committee hearings, especially investigative hearings, sometimes provide suitable moments. But many day-to-day legislative processes, even those processes that are open to camera coverage, are visually unexciting.

b. Network news executives believe the networks have overfocused on Washington, which has hurt congressional coverage, according to one correspondent. The trend now is to cover policy issues from a location elsewhere in the country, where the policy is relevant, rather than from Capitol Hill or the White House.

c. Two elements of the news in general apply with special weight to television, making the multifaceted complexity of Congress particularly difficult to explain.

i. Simplicity. A newspaper reader can reread a complex paragraph; a television viewer cannot go back and review something he missed.

ii. Brevity. A newspaper reader can skip something he already knows or doesn't care about; a television viewer must sit through one story to reach the next one.

B. *Media's Effects on Congress*
　1. Systemic level
　　a. Agenda-setting. Media's role in working with other players in order to promote particular issues.
　　b. Relative importance of institutions. What Robinson posits for television is presumably applicable to newspapers as well: "Television alters the popularly perceived importance of institutions and individuals in direct proportion to the amount of coverage provided—the greater the coverage, the more important the institution and its members appear to be." [Robinson (b) 252]
　　c. The public's view of institutions as good or bad, effective or ineffective. Miller et al. found a correlation between the negative tone of newspaper coverage and citizen views of the institutions covered. "Apparently, the public's evaluations of government performance flow rather directly from the image of the political process as seen through the prism of newspaper reporting." [81]
　2. Institutional level
　Most of the following points concern the national media. As noted above, though, not all members court the national media.
　　a. Media attention per se can affect the bargaining process. Publicity that a party leader or White House official is pressuring a member may incline the member to hang tough. Or, when word gets out that a member received a particular reward (e.g., a water project in his district) in exchange for a vote, other members will be encouraged to demand as much or more for their votes.
　　b. It seems that Congressmen now undertake greater efforts to attract national coverage than they have in years past, the above caveats notwithstanding. The sense of relative deprivation vis-a-vis the White House is probably one factor. So is the decentralization of congressional authority, permitting if not encouraging each member to fend for himself, with the media as elsewhere.
　　If this is true, then the business of Congress falls on fewer and fewer members—for, as Mayhew writes, "[T]he hero of the Hill is not the hero of the airwaves. The member who earns prestige among his peers is

the lonely gnome who passes up news conferences, cocktail parties, sometimes even marriage in order to devote his time to legislative 'homework.' " [147] Thus, as members pay increasing attention to the national media, Congress itself suffers.

c. In order to attract additional coverage, Congress has opened up some of its processes to the media, mainly television. Cameras have been permitted in committee rooms and the House.

There is a logic—cynical but demonstrable—behind this, suggesting that reducing the costs the media incur in gathering news may increase the institution's share of the news. To date, no one has published any study of Congress's share of the network news since television entered the House. According to Bruce Collins of C-SPAN, the congressional share of the news has remained roughly the same; however, film of members being interviewed in hallways has been replaced, by and large, by film of floor speeches.

d. Congress has not only exposed its behavior, it has altered its behavior in order to attract coverage.
   i. As cited previously, Robinson and Appel found that network news coverage focused largely on investigative hearings. That, they argue, has encouraged Congress to shift "its incentive structure even farther away from legislation or legislative hearings and moving more and more toward media-dominated, investigative hearings." [416-17] One near-staple of hearings seeking coverage is testimony by celebrities. A 1983 hearing on televising the Senate featured testimony from Walter Cronkite and George Will, attracting a brace of network cameras, and prompting one senator to remark: "I made mention as I passed the press a few moments ago, that we really had them out today, and they let me know right quick that I did not get them out today, that the witnesses got them out today. And so I am very proud that they are here, and we have all these cameras. I invite them to come to the Energy Committee as we begin our debate on the deregulation of natural gas. If we could have this kind of a group of cam-

eras in that committee hearing, I think the consumers of this country might understand the deregulation of natural gas issue better." [U.S. Senate 2]

ii. Similarly, coverage can encourage members to make inflammatory statements, in order to get on the news or in newspapers. Certainly political hyperbole is nothing new. But it has been argued that television cameras in particular sometimes generate it when it otherwise wouldn't be present. At the hearings on televising the Senate, Senator Dennis DeConcini said: "Now, I have been on committees and seen Senators who have all the earmarks of statesmanship, with those cameras in that room, proceed to get up and make vitriolic statements of a very controversial nature that are not appropriate for the hearing at all—the sort of things I have never seen those Senators do in a dozen years. Why? Because the television cameras are there. . . ." [U.S. Senate 22]

iii. The desire for press coverage can also encourage members or committees to become issue entrepreneurs. As Miller writes, "[T]he only way to get covered is to become the best and most complete source of information about a topic already being covered or to pick a topic that is more 'newsworthy' (negative, unexpected, elite or unambiguous) than the topic the President is pushing." [Miller (b) 464]

iv. Obviously some issues, although important, will not attract heavy press coverage; the press incentive system will tend to discourage members from devoting time and attention to such issues. (Other incentives exist too, naturally; the question is their relative power.)

e. As some activities become more important, others become less important. For example, the press tends to give a member's position and rhetoric on a bill; it seldom follows the issue through complex hearings and votes, taking note throughout of the member's efforts, if any, to shape or pass the bill. Thus, Mayhew argues, even members who have taken strong positions lack the press or electoral incentive to care whether most bills pass, with the important exception of bills providing "particularized benefits" for the member's constituents. On busing legislation, Mayhew writes, "The Detroit congressmen had every reason to worry about whether they were voting on the right side but no reason to worry about what passed or was implemented. The electoral payment was purely for positions taken. Of course congressmen must at all times generate an impression that they are interested in winning victories, but there may not be much behind the impression." [15]

f. For members seeking press attention, the incentive is to get on certain committees. "There are, it appears, some Congressmen who want to serve on whatever committees happen to be dealing with the most pressing, controversial, national problems of the time," Fenno found. [Fenno (a) 10] Foreign Affairs, for instance, "provides an obvious platform where members can talk knowingly about matters of war and peace, thus increasing their visibility, acquiring statesmanlike reputations, and enlarging their geopolitical boundaries." [13] More mundane committees, consequently, may have trouble getting the enthusiastic attention of their members. Further, members of the high-visibility committees may use them principally as platforms and pay less attention to committee business per se. Chairman Fulbright of Foreign Relations said: "This is the kind of committee that Senators like to be on, but they don't like to do anything." [Mayhew 123]

g. Media attention on a particular issue, bill, or hearing can change the legislative outcome, as Mayhew writes. He recounts the auto safety hearings in the House Commerce Committee—which would normally be expected to side with the automakers—and quotes David Price's conclusion: "The reason it did not behave in this fashion can be summarized in a single word: publicity." [177] According to one lobbyist, the *Washington Post* often editorializes on an issue the day that it's scheduled to be voted on in sub-

committee; sometimes that is enough to determine a fence-sitter's vote.
- h. Using the moment's hot issue to attract coverage can raise problems for members, who may be encouraged to make strong statements early on, when an issue is fresh and spokespeople are few. Later, with the benefit of time and additional information, they may want to change position, but find it difficult to do so.
- i. Purely as information, news coverage shapes congressional perceptions. As Sigal writes: "On most matters outside the immediate purview of his committees, he relies for his information and his cues to voting on others. . . . In a body with such a diversity of backgrounds, representing such a variety of electoral districts, one common ground is the reliance on a rather small number of organizations for their news. This reliance makes the Congress more susceptible to leadership by the sources of news at the other end of Pennsylvania Avenue." [183]
- j. For electoral reasons, some members intentionally bait the national media as an appeal to voters ("the man who stood up to the *Washington Post*").

C. *Congress's Problems with the Media*
1. Aspects of press performance that sometimes hinder members' efforts:
   a. Press's failure, frequently, to provide perspective, history, background.
   b. Press often misses coalitions on legislation, and who wins and loses down the road.
   c. Press's failure, frequently, to dig for the truth about conflicting information. Wrong information is rarely disproved by the reporter; usually it's run alongside a rebuttal from someone else, with no effort to resolve the difference (e.g., the number killed in Lebanon, the potential impact on prices of gas deregulation). The member who knows his information is correct will be frustrated by knee-jerk objectivity.
   d. Truth about hyperbole seldom comes through in the press. Those seeking coverage often compete to make the most colorful, extreme statements concerning the importance of the issue and the costs of a wrong decision. The press rarely questions such statements.

e. Laziness. Tendency for reporter to ask an author to summarize his study instead of reading it. Reporters often fail to keep up with trade press in a given area (e.g., defense, business) which could provide important information.
f. Pack journalism.
g. Competition. Sometimes this amounts to the opposite of pack journalism—a tendency to avoid, or to dig for the other side of, an issue the competition grabbed first.

2. Aspects of press performance that almost always hinder members' efforts:
   a. A frequent negative slant to coverage of Congress.
      i. This is endemic to news in general. It may occur partly because, according to several studies, reporters personally tend to look down on the politicians they cover, and thus may look for news that confirms their preconceptions.
      ii. In story selection, this means that scandals, junkets, and instances of congressional blundering tend to become news.
      iii. In story tone, this means that the news sometimes seems to reflect what David Broder calls reporters' "air of moral superiority." The media sometimes push to make political issues into ethical issues (e.g., financial disclosure of members, or Freedom of Information). Sometimes they seem to view "compromise" as a pejorative term; legislators view it as an imperative. And the media frequently denigrate various aspects—commonplace and arguably essential—of the process, such as lobbying, vote-trading, and member travel.
      iv. Also, it seems to result in a strong emphasis on money, and a tendency to view potential corruption, such as a link between a PAC contribution and a subsequent vote, as genuine corruption without further investigation. A recent study by two economists found a stronger causal relationship between ideology/constituent needs and votes, than between contributions and votes. But, as Paul Taylor writes, "money can be tracked with real live numbers, which

working reporters cling to as lifeboats on a sea of ambiguity." [A9] Also, proving that a contribution influenced a subsequent vote is exceedingly difficult, often impossible; instead reporters usually point out the potential or apparent influence.
- b. Invasions of members' privacy.
- c. Difficult to get inaccurate or misleading stories corrected.
- d. Press often fails to give appropriate attention to members' districts. The member may vote against party or ideology in favor of constituents; the press often fails to pick up on that. The national press tends to apply a single standard to all members, without considering how such a stance might legitimately jibe with district needs and interests. Some reporters justify that, as a search for statesmen with national perspective. To what extent is that explanation true or valid?

  In general, the national media tend to ignore, or to treat negatively, members' reelection imperative and its various manifestations:
  - i. District focus of attention.
  - ii. Casework and mail.
  - iii. Efforts to gauge district opinion.
  - iv. Efforts to show constituents how the member has represented their needs and interests.
  - v. Tendency for member to emphasize the importance of seniority in persuading voters to return the incumbent to office.
  - vi. Role of staff in reelection effort, often sub rosa.
  - vii. Role of lobbying and PAC contributions in reelection.
- e. Tendency at the national level to ignore press releases—because so many, because viewed as self-serving.
- f. Sense among some players that the national press, in its story selection and coverage, is persistently liberal. True or false, this perception guides the way that some players deal with or around the press.

D. *Congress's Effects on the Media*
  1. The institutional complexity, mentioned above, makes Congress exceedingly difficult to cover.
  2. Reporters cover what they can cover. Newsworthy events

won't be covered if they occur behind closed doors and no one will talk. In general, though, countervailing incentives exist. If a member in favor of a particular bill wants to keep it quiet, the bill's opponents will probably want publicity.

3. Coverage depends upon the openness, knowledge, and veracity of sources. If the workhorses won't talk, reporters will have to rely on showhorses who may not know the full story.
4. Generally, reporters enjoy a relatively chummy relationship with members, in contrast to the often-formal relationship with administration officials.
5. Reporters want to maintain helpful sources, and so they have an incentive in some instances to protect cooperative members.
6. Similarly, reporters have an incentive to go along with sources' wishes (e.g., not for attribution, embargo). Among other things, this means that the importance of congressional staff often doesn't come through in coverage; staffers, valuable sources to many reporters, generally request anonymity.
7. Reporters sometimes work closely with congressional committees, sharing information in exchange for exclusives.
8. Fear of libel sometimes causes investigative reporters to tie their stories to congressional study or action, according to Miller. "[M]any of their topics—scandal, misconduct—were prime candidates for libel suits. Being able to say a committee had something under investigation or to quote a committee report provided a certain amount of protection." [Miller (a) 660]

VI. OTHER QUESTIONS

A. A member's district or state media often treat him as the conduit between the constituency and the federal government. As such, the local media rely on him, to an extent, for information and interpretation of government actions. But the local media must also treat him as a politician seeking reelection, frequently one of several aspirants for the seat he now occupies. Can these two needs be resolved adequately, in terms of the member, his opponents in the election, and the voter?

B. Public opinion surveys have found widespread ignorance concerning the workings of Congress. If this is the case, should the media try harder to explain congressional processes? Would that bore or alienate more sophisticated readers, possibly without attracting the less informed and less interested?

C. Reporters often rely heavily on congressional staff. Staffers frequently specialize, and thus are more informed on specifics than the member; also, staffers are frequently more accessible to reporters. For several reasons, including a desire not to overshadow the member, a staffer frequently will provide information only on background. Do readers and viewers, as a consequence, gain a misleading impression of reporters' sources? Do they fail to understand the importance of congressional staff?

D. What are the trade-offs entailed in choosing a reporter to cover Congress? Is a political generalist or an issue specialist better? Are there advantages to shifting assignments periodically, or is it better to rely on a reporter with years of Hill experience?

E. As Haskell found, more and more members are working to bypass the press via cablecasts, satellite feeds, and older methods such as press releases to local media and newsletters to voters. Should the presence of this alternative conduit influence media coverage of Congress?

F. Should reporters get involved in the process? Should they trade information with a committee investigating a topic? If they do, should they reveal that fact in their coverage?

G. How should reporters cover legislative issues affecting the media? How should they treat, for example, Katharine Graham's lobbying of members to prohibit the phone company from starting "electronic yellow pages" that might reduce newspaper classified-ad revenue?

H. How should the media treat obvious media events—e.g., a Senate committee's dining on food taken from supermarket dumpsters, in order to dramatize the problem of food waste?

I. Are there special media events questions applicable to newspaper photographers and to television? To make the point that a tax-cut amendment introduced by a Senate Democrat was, in fact, virtually identical to the Republicans' Roth-Kemp bill, a group of Republicans held a press conference and passed out cigars, celebrating the birth of the "Son of Roth-Kemp." The incident made network news, and a photo of the members and their cigars made the front page of the *Washington Post*. Chris Wallace of NBC said, "Had they held a straight, conservative, respectable news conference, they wouldn't have gotten any attention at all." [A. Taylor, 37]

BIBLIOGRAPHY

Bagdikian, Ben H. "Congress and the Media: Partners in Propaganda." In Robert O. Blanchard, ed., *Congress and the News Media, op. cit.*, pp. 388-398.

Balutis, Alan P. "Congress, the President and the Press." *Journalism Quarterly* (53) (1976), pp. 509-515.

Blanchard, Robert O., ed., *Congress and the News Media.* New York: Hastings House Publishers, 1974.

Cater, Douglass. *The Fourth Branch of Government.* New York: Vintage, 1965, orig. publ. 1959.

Clarke, Peter, and Eric Fredin. "Newspapers, Television and Political Reasoning." *Public Opinion Quarterly* (1978), pp. 143-160.

Cornwell, Elmer E., Jr. "Presidential News: The Expanding Public Image." *Journalism Quarterly* (1959), pp. 275-283.

Epstein, Edward Jay. *News from Nowhere: Television and the News.* New York: Vintage, 1974.

Fenno, Richard F., Jr. (a). *Congressmen in Committees.* Boston: Little, Brown, 1973.

Fenno, Richard F., Jr. (b). "If, as Ralph Nader says, Congress is 'the Broken Branch,' How Come We Love Our Congressmen So Much?" In Norman Ornstein, ed., *Congress in Change, op. cit.*, pp. 277-287.

Fulbright, J. William. "Fulbright on the Press." *Columbia Journalism Review*, November/December 1975, pp. 39-45.

Gans, Herbert J. *Deciding What's News : A Study of CBS Evening News, NBC Nightly News, Newsweek, and Time.* New York: Vintage, 1979.

Graber, Doris A. *Mass Media and American Politics.* Washington: Congressional Quarterly Press, 1980.

Haskell, Anne. "Live from Capitol Hill: Where Politicians Use High Tech to Bypass the Press." *Washington Journalism Review*, November 1982, pp. 48-50.

Mayhew, David R. *Congress: The Electoral Connection.* New Haven, Conn.: Yale University Press, 1974.

Miller, Arthur H., Edie N. Goldenberg, and Lutz Erbring. "Type-Set Politics: Impact of Newspapers on Public Confidence." *American Political Science Review* (73) (1979), pp. 67-84.

Miller, Susan H. (a). "Congressional Committee Hearings and the Media: Rules of the Game." *Journalism Quarterly* (55) (1978), pp. 657-663.

Miller, Susan H. (b). "News Coverage of Congress: The Search for the Ultimate Spokesman." *Journalism Quarterly* (54) (1977), pp. 459-465.

Ornstein, Norman, ed. *Congress in Change.* New York: Praeger, 1975.

Polk, Leslie D., John Eddy, and Ann Andre. "Use of Congressional Publicity in a Wisconsin District." *Journalism Quarterly* (52) (1975), pp. 543-546.

Reed, Leonard. "The Bureaucracy: The Cleverest Lobby of Them All." *Washington Monthly*, April 1978, pp. 49-54.

Robinson, Michael J. (a). "Public Affairs Television and the Growth of Political Malaise: The Case of 'The Selling of the Pentagon.'" *American Political Science Review* (70) (1976), pp. 409-432.

Robinson, Michael J. (b). "A Twentieth-Century Medium in a Nineteenth-Century Legislature: The Effects of Television on the American Congress." In Norman Orstein, ed., *Congress in Change, op. cit.*, pp. 240-261.

Robinson, Michael J., and Kevin R. Appel. "Network News Coverage of Congress." *Political Science Quarterly* (94) (1979), pp. 407-418.

Robinson, Michael J., and Maura E. Clancey. "King of the Hill: When It Comes to News, Congress Turns to the Washington Post." *Washington Journalism Review*, July/August 1983, pp. 46-49.

Sigal, Leon V. *Reporters and Officials: The Organization and Politics of Newsmaking.* Lexington, Mass.: Heath, 1973.

Taylor, Adrian C. "The Flacks of the Hill." *Washington Journalism Review*, June/July 1979, pp. 36-44.

Taylor, Paul. "Lobbyists' Success at Raising Funds Proves Costly." *Washington Post*, August 2, 1983, pp. A1, A9.

U.S. Senate. Committee on Rules and Administration. "Hearings to Establish Regulations to Implement Television and Radio Coverage of Proceedings of the Senate," April 14-15, 1983. Washington: Government Printing Office, 1983.

JK 1140 .M43 1987

DATE DUE		
DEC - 4 1992		
JUL 1 3 2000		